Coastal Plain Community Tree Guide:
Benefits, Costs, and Strategic Planting

November 2006

E. Gregory McPherson[1]
James R. Simpson[1]
Paula J. Peper[1]
Shelley L. Gardner[1]
Kelaine E. Vargas[1]
Scott E. Maco[1]
Qingfu Xiao[2]

[1]Center for Urban Forest Research
USDA Forest Service
Pacific Southwest Research Station
Davis, CA

[2]Department of Land, Air, and Water Resources
University of California, Davis

Contributing Organizations

Center for Urban Forest Research
USDA Forest Service, Pacific Southwest Research Station
Davis, CA

Department of Land, Air, and Water Resources
University of California
Davis, CA

Sponsoring Organization

USDA Forest Service
State and Private Forestry
Urban and Community Forestry Program

Acknowledgements

We appreciate the assistance provided by Danny Burbage (Urban Forestry Superintendent, City of Charleston, SC); Greg Ina, Jim Jenkins, and Karen Wise (Davey Resource Group); John L. Schrenk (SC Dept. of Health & Environmental Control); Jason Caldwell and Wes Tyler (SC Dept. of Natural Resources); Michael Merritt (Texas Forest Service); Wendee Holtcamp (Freelance Writer & Photographer); Ilya Bezdezhskiy, Stephanie Louie, and Stephanie Huang (CUFR); and Sam Dunn (for many of the photographs included in this publication).

Tree care expenditure information was provided by Danny Burbage (City of Charleston, SC), Bill Haws (City of Savannah, GA), Don Robertson (City of Jacksonville, FL), Dudley Hartel (USDA Forest Service), Jed Day (Davey Tree), Mike Russell (Russell Consulting, LLC), Michael Merritt (Texas Forest Service), Charles Burditt and Jack Hill (Burditt Sustainable Natural Resource Consultants).

Dr. Timothy Broschat (University of Florida, Ft. Lauderdale), Joe Le Vert (Southeastern Palm Society), and Ollie Oliver (Palm Trees, Ltd.) provided valuable assistance with calculating palm tree growth.

Neil Letson (State Urban Forestry Coordinator, Alabama Cooperative Extension) and Dr. Kamran Abdollahi (Professor, Southern University Urban Forestry Program) provided helpful reviews of this work.

Mark Buscaino, Ed Macie (USDA Forest Service, State and Private Forestry), and Liz Gilland (U&CF Program Coordinator SC Forestry Commission) provided invaluable support for this project.

What's in This Tree Guide?

This tree guide is organized as follows:

Executive Summary: Presents key findings.

Chapter 1: Describes the Guide's purpose, audience, and geographic scope.

Chapter 2: Provides background information on the potential of trees in Coastal Plain communities to provide benefits and describes management costs that are typically incurred.

Chapter 3: Provides calculations of tree benefits and costs for the Coastal Plain region.

Chapter 4: Illustrates how to estimate urban forest benefits and costs for tree planting projects in your community and offers tips to increase cost-effectiveness.

Chapter 5: Presents guidelines for selecting and placing trees in residential yards and public open spaces.

Appendix A: Suggests additional resources for further information.

Appendix B: Contains tables that list annual benefits and costs of representative tree species at 5-year intervals for 40 years after planting.

Appendix B: Describes the methods, assumptions, and limitations associated with estimating tree benefits.

Glossary of terms: Provides definitions for technical terms used in the report.

References: Lists references cited in the guide.

This guide will help users quantify the long-term benefits and costs associated with proposed tree planting projects. It is also available online at http://www.fs.fed.us/psw/programs/cufr/.

The Center for Urban Forest Research (CUFR) has developed a computer program called STRATUM to estimate the benefits and costs for existing street and park trees. STRATUM is part of the i-Tree software suite. More information on i-Tree and STRATUM is available at http://www.itreetools.org and http://www.fs.fed.us/psw/programs/cufr/.

Table of Contents

In the Coastal Plain region, trees play an environmental, cultural, and historical role in communities. Charleston's Angel Oak, a Southern live oak estimated to be more than 1,000 years old, is pictured here.

Executive Summary

This report quantifies benefits and costs for representative large, medium, and small broadleaf trees and coniferous trees in the Coastal Plain region: the species chosen as representative are the Southern live oak (*Quercus virginiana*), Southern magnolia (*Magnolia grandiflora*), flowering dogwood (*Cornus florida*), and loblolly pine (*Pinus taeda*), respectively. The analysis describes "yard trees" (those planted in residential sites) and "public trees" (those planted on streets or in parks). Benefits are calculated using tree growth curves and numerical models that consider regional climate, building characteristics, air pollutant concentrations, and prices. Tree care costs and mortality rates are based on results from a survey of municipal and commercial arborists. We assume a 65% survival rate over a 40-year time frame.

Benefits and costs quantified

The measurements used in modeling environmental and other benefits of trees are based on in-depth research carried out for Charleston, South Carolina. Given the Coastal Plain region's broad and diverse geographical area, this approach provides first-order approximations. It is a general accounting that can be easily adapted and adjusted for local planting projects. Two examples are provided that illustrate how to adjust benefits and costs to reflect different aspects of local planting projects.

Adjusting values for local planting projects

Large trees provide the most benefits. Average annual benefits increase with mature tree size and vary based on tree location. The lowest values are for yard trees on the southern side of houses and the highest values are for yard trees on east or west sides of houses. Values for public trees are intermediate. Benefits range as follows:

Annual benefits

- $107 to $127 for a large tree
- $31 to $40 for a medium tree
- $14 to $19 for a small tree
- $50 to $62 for a conifer

Benefits associated with reducing stormwater runoff and energy use and increased aesthetic and other benefits reflected in increased property values account for the largest proportion of total benefits in this region. Reduced levels of air pollutants and carbon dioxide in the air are the next most important benefits.

Energy conservation benefits vary with tree location as well as size. Trees located opposite east- and west-facing walls provide the greatest net heating and cooling energy savings. Reducing heating and cooling energy needs reduces carbon dioxide emissions and thereby reduces atmospheric carbon dioxide. Similarly, energy savings that reduce pollutant emissions at power plants account for important reductions in gases that produce ozone, a major component of smog.

Costs

The benefits of trees are offset by the costs of caring for them. The average annual costs for tree care range from $10 to $23 per tree. (Values below are for yard and public trees, respectively.)

- **$19** and **$23** for a large tree
- **$15** and **$18** for a medium tree
- **$12** and **$14** for a small tree
- **$10** and **$14** for a conifer

Pruning is the greatest cost associated with broadleaf trees ($4 to $10 per tree per year). Planting costs, annualized over 40 years, are the next highest expense ($4 to $5 per tree per year).

Average annual net benefits

Average annual net benefits (benefits minus costs) per tree for a 40-year period vary by tree location and tree size and range from a low of $1 to a high of $108 per tree.

- Large tree: **$87** for a yard tree on the south side of a house to **$108** for a yard tree on the east or west sides of a house
- Medium tree: **$16** for a yard tree on the south side of a house to **$26** for a yard tree on the east or west sides of a house
- Small tree: **$1** for a public tree to **$7** for a yard tree on the east or west sides of a house
- Conifer: **$40** for a yard tree on the south side of a house to **$51** for a yard tree on the east or west sides of a house

Environmental benefits alone, including energy savings, stormwater runoff reduction, improved air quality, and reduced atmospheric carbon dioxide, are up to six times greater than tree care costs.

Net benefits summed for 40 years

Net benefits for a yard tree opposite a west wall and a public tree are substantial for larger species when summed over the entire 40-year period (values below are for yard trees opposite a west wall and public trees, respectively):

- $4,320 and $3,880 for a large tree
- $1,040 and $760 for a medium tree
- $280 and $40 for a small tree
- $2,040 and $1,640 for a conifer

Yard trees produce higher net benefits than public trees, primarily because of lower maintenance costs.

To demonstrate ways that communities can adapt the information in this report to their needs, two fictional cities interested in improving their urban forest have been created. The benefits and costs of different planting projects are determined. In the hypothetical city of Cypress Creek, net benefits and benefit–cost ratios (BCRs; total benefits divided by costs) are calculated for a planting of 1,000 trees (1-inch) assuming a cost of $120 per tree, 65% survival rate, and 40-year analysis. Total costs are $823,820, benefits total $3,997,165, and net benefits are $3,173,345 ($79.33 per tree per year). The BCR is 4.85:1, indicating that $4.85 is returned for every $1 invested. The net benefits and BCRs (in parentheses) by mature tree size are:

Adjusting for local planting projects

- $2,865,706 (5.53:1) for 700 large trees

- $128,159 (2.19:1) for 150 medium trees

- $4,048 (1.15:1) for 50 small trees

- $175,432 (4.12:1) for 100 conifer trees

Stormwater benefits (28%) and increased property values reflecting aesthetic and other benefits of trees (46%) account for about three-quarters of the estimated benefits. Reduced energy costs (23%), and atmospheric CO_2 reduction (3%) make up the remaining benefits.

In the fictional city of Tillandsia, long-term planting and tree care costs and benefits were compared to determine if a proposed policy that favors planting small trees would be cost-effective compared to the current policy of planting large trees where space permits. Over a 40-year period, the net benefits are:

- $3,804 per tree for a live oak

- $719 per tree for a Southern magnolia

- $23 per tree for a dogwood

Based on this analysis, the city of Tillandsia decided to retain its policy. Developers are now required to create tree shade plans that show how they will achieve 50% shade over streets, sidewalks, and parking lots within 15 years of development.

The green infrastructure is a significant component of communities in the Coastal Plain region.

Chapter 1. Introduction

From small towns surrounded by cropland, forests, and the sea, to Houston, the nation's fourth largest city, the Coastal Plain region (*Figure 1*) contains a diverse assemblage of communities that are home to approximately 10 million people. The region extends in a narrow coastal band from eastern Texas along the Gulf Coast across the panhandle of Florida and north along the Atlantic Coast to southern North Carolina (*Figure 1*). Boundaries correspond with Sunset Climate Zones 28 and part of 29 (Brenzel 2001) and USDA Hardiness Zones 8 and 9. The **climate*** in this region ranges from mild in southeastern North Carolina to subtropical along the Gulf. Temperatures rarely fall below freezing, allowing a great number of tree species to thrive. Summers are hot and humid, though winds off the ocean and the Gulf of Mexico provide some relief. Annual precipitation ranges from 50 to 70 inches (1,200–1,800 mm) and falls fairly evenly throughout the year (Ning et al. 2003).

Coastal Plain communities can derive many benefits from community trees

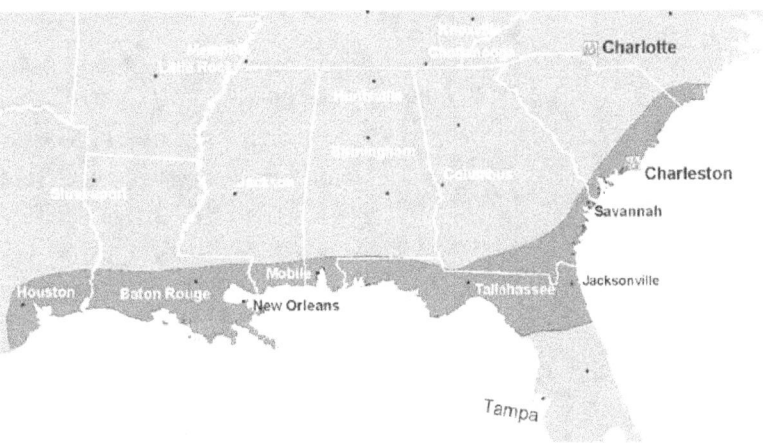

Figure 1. *The Coastal Plain region (shaded area) extends in a narrow coastal band from eastern Texas along the Coastal Plain across the panhandle of Florida and north along the Atlantic Coast to southern North Carolina. Charleston, South Carolina, is the reference city for this region.*

The Coastal Plain region is characterized by flat, low-lying coastal areas. Rivers and streams are common, and wetlands play a critical role in the ecosystem, accommodating flood waters, cleaning stormwater runoff, and providing a vital habitat for wildlife and a nursery for many marine species. The wetlands vary in character and may be forested, including swamps, mangroves, and pocosins, or unforested, including marshes, mudflats and natural ponds, such as Carolina Bays (Ning et al. 2003; McNab and Avers 1994). Long, narrow barrier islands line the coast in many areas, buffering the mainland. Soils vary from the extremely rich alluvium of the Mississippi Delta to the arid, acidic sandy soils of the barrier islands.

The tree cover of the Coastal Plain is also quite varied and includes oak-hickory-pine forest with deciduous and evergreen hardwoods, such as red maple (*Acer rubrum*), hickory (*Carya* spp.), water (*Quercus nigra*) and live oaks (*Q. virginiana*), sweetgum (*Liquidambar styraciflua*) and blackgum (*Nyssa sylvatica*); and evergreen and deciduous needle-leaved trees, such as bald and pond cypress (*Taxodium distichum*) as well as longleaf (*Pinus palustris*), loblolly (*P. taeda*),

*Bold-faced words are defined in the Glossary.

pond (*P. serotina*), and slash pines (*P. elliottii*). Most of the area was once cleared for agriculture and the existing forest is second-growth.

Hurricanes are a fact of life for Coastal Plain communities. These natural events can become human disasters. Hurricane Katrina emphasized the link between human and environmental systems when levees broke and New Orleans flooded. Accompanying the loss of approximately 250,000 structures and 1,000 lives was the destruction of many city trees that shaded streets, cleaned the air, increased property values and enhanced quality of life. Tornados spawned by hurricanes and summer storms also impact Coastal Plain communities. Seeing favorite trees toppled or badly damaged can be a traumatic shock to residents. However, experience suggests that many trees will recover with time because of their amazing resilience. The Urban Forestry South Web site (www.urbanforestrysouth.org) has a wealth of information on storm recovery and assistance.

Quality of life improves with trees

As the communities of the Coastal Plain continue to grow and change during the coming decades, sustaining healthy community forests is integral to the quality of life residents experience. In the Coastal Plain region, urban forest canopies form living umbrellas. They are distinctive features of the landscape that protect us from the elements, clean the water we drink and the air we breathe, and form a connection to earlier generations who planted and tended these trees.

Trees provide environmental benefits

The role of urban forests in enhancing the environment, increasing community attractiveness and livability, and fostering civic pride takes on greater significance as communities strive to balance economic growth with environmental quality and social well-being. The simple act of planting trees provides opportunities to connect residents with nature and with each other. Neighborhood tree plantings and stewardship projects stimulate investment by local citizens, businesses, and governments for the betterment of their communities (*Figure 2*). Community forests bring opportunity for economic renewal, combating development woes, and increasing the quality of life for community residents.

Coastal Plain communities can promote energy efficiency through tree planting and stewardship programs that strategi-

Figure 2. Tree planting and stewardship programs provide opportunities for local residents to work together to build better communities.

cally locate trees to save energy and minimize conflicts with urban infrastructure. The same trees can provide additional benefits by reducing stormwater runoff; improving local air, soil, and water quality; reducing atmospheric carbon dioxide (CO_2); providing wildlife habitat; increasing property values; slowing traffic; enhancing community attractiveness and investment; and promoting human well-being.

This guide builds upon studies by the USDA Forest Service in Chicago and Sacramento (McPherson et al. 1994, 1997), American Forest's urban ecosystem analyses in New Orleans and Montgomery, AL (American Forests 2002, 2004), a Texas Forest Service and USDA Forest Service study of the trees in Houston (Smith et al. 2005) and other regional Tree Guides from the Center for Urban Forest Research (McPherson et al. 1999a, 2000, 2003, 2005a, 2006b) to extend knowledge of urban forest benefits in the Coastal Plain. The guide:

- Quantifies benefits of trees on a per-tree basis rather than on a **canopy cover** basis (it should not be used to estimate benefits for trees growing in forest stands).

- Describes management costs and benefits.

- Details how tree planting programs can improve environmental quality, conserve energy, and add value to communities.

- Explains where residential yard and public trees should be placed to maximize their benefits and cost-effectiveness.

- Describes ways conflicts between trees and power lines, sidewalks, and buildings can be minimized.

- Illustrates how to use this information to estimate benefits and costs for local tree planting projects.

What will this tree guide do?

These guidelines are specific to the Coastal Plain, and based on data and calculations from open-growing urban trees in this region.

Street, park, and shade trees are components of all Coastal Plain communities, and they impact every resident. Their benefits are myriad. However, with municipal tree programs dependent on taxpayer-supported general funds, communities are forced to ask whether trees are worth the price to plant and care for over the long term, thus requiring urban forestry programs to demonstrate their cost-effectiveness (McPherson 1995). If tree plantings are proven to benefit communities, then monetary commitment to tree programs will be justified. Therefore, the objective of this tree guide is to identify and describe the benefits and costs of planting trees in Coastal Plain communities—providing a tool for municipal tree managers, arborists, and tree enthusiasts to increase public awareness and support for trees (Dwyer and Miller 1999).

Audience and objective

Trees in Coastal Plain communities enhance quality of life.

Chapter 2. Identifying Benefits and Costs of Urban and Community Forests

This chapter describes benefits and costs of public and privately managed trees. The functional benefits and associated economic value of community forests are presented. Expenditures related to tree care and management are assessed—a necessary process for creating cost-effective programs (Hudson 1983, Dwyer et al. 1992).

Benefits

Saving Energy

Energy is an essential ingredient for quality of life and for economic growth. Conserving energy by greening our cities is often more cost-effective than building new power plants. For example, while California was experiencing energy shortages in 2001, its 177 million city trees were providing shade and conserving energy. Annual savings to utilities were an estimated $500 million in wholesale electricity and generation purchases (McPherson and Simpson 2003). Planting 50 million more shade trees in strategic locations would provide savings equivalent to seven 100-megawatt power plants. The cost of peak load reduction was $63/kW, considerably less than the $150/kW benchmark for cost-effectiveness. A recent study of Houston's regional urban forest suggests that Houston's trees save approximately $111.8 million in annual air conditioning costs and $13.9 million in heating costs (Smith et al. 2005). Utilities in the Coastal Plain and throughout the country can invest in shade tree programs as a cost-effective energy conservation measure.

Trees modify climate and conserve building energy use in three principal ways (*Figure 3*):

- Shading reduces the amount of heat absorbed and stored by built surfaces.

- **Evapotranspiration** converts liquid water to water vapor and thus cools the air by using solar energy that would otherwise result in heating of the air.

How trees work to save energy

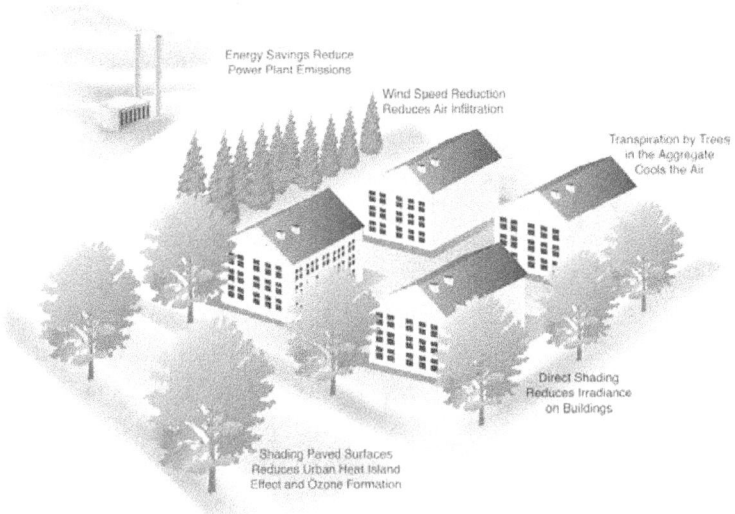

Figure 3. Trees save energy for heating and cooling by shading buildings, lowering summertime temperatures, and reducing wind speeds. Secondary benefits from energy conservation are reduced water consumption and reduced pollutant emissions by power plants (drawing by Mike Thomas).

- Reducing wind speed reduces the infiltration of outside air into interior spaces and heat loss, especially where conductivity is relatively high (e.g., glass windows) (Simpson 1998).

Trees lower temperatures

Trees and other vegetation on individual building sites may lower air temperatures 5°F (3°C) compared with outside the **greenspace**. At larger scales (6 square miles [10 km²]), temperature differences of more than 9°F (5°C) have been observed between city centers and more vegetated suburban areas (Akbari et al. 1992). These "hot spots" in cities are called **urban heat islands**.

For individual buildings, strategically placed trees can increase energy efficiency in the summer and winter. Because the summer sun is low in the east and west for several hours each day, solar angles should be considered. Trees that shade east, and especially, west walls help keep buildings cool (*Figure 4*). In the winter, allowing the sun to strike the southern side of a building can warm interior spaces. However, the trunks and bare branches of **deciduous** trees that shade south- and east-facing walls during winter may increase heating costs by blocking 40% or more of winter sun (McPherson 1984).

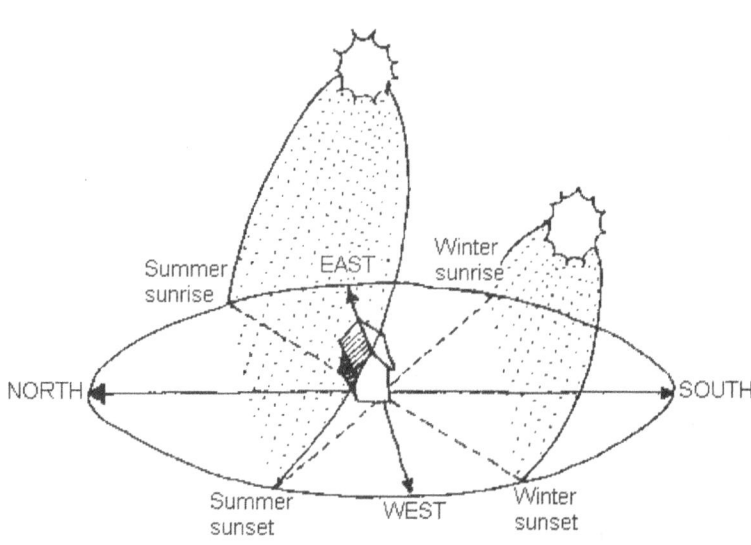

Figure 4. Paths of the sun on winter and summer solstices (from Sand 1991). Summer heat gain is primarily through east- and west-facing windows and walls. The roof receives most irradiance, but insulated attics reduce heat gain to living spaces. The winter sun, at a lower angle, strikes the south-facing surfaces.

Windbreaks reduce heat loss

Rates at which outside air infiltrates a building can increase substantially with wind speed. In cold, windy weather, the entire volume of air, even in newer or tightly sealed homes, may change every two to three hours. Windbreaks reduce wind speed and resulting air infiltration by up to 50%, translating into potential annual heating savings of 10–12% (Heisler 1986). Reductions in wind speed reduce heat transfer through conductive materials as well. Cool winter winds, blowing against windows, can contribute significantly to the heating load of buildings by increasing the temperature gradient between inside and outside temperatures. Windbreaks reduce air infiltration and conductive heat loss from buildings.

Trees can save money

Trees provide greater energy savings in the Coastal Plain than in cooler climate regions because they reduce air conditioning loads during the hot, humid summers. In Atlanta, for example, trees were found to produce substantial cooling savings for an energy efficient two-story wood-frame house (McPherson et al. 1993). A computer simulation of annual cooling savings indicated that the typical household with air conditioning spends about $225 each year for cooling. Shade and lower air temperatures from three 25-ft tall (7.5 m) trees—two on the west side of the house and one on the east—were estimated to save $77 each year for cooling, a 34% reduction (1,035 kWh). Conserving energy by greening our cities is important because it can be more cost-effective than building new power plants (see "Green Plants or Power Plants?" and "Save Dollars with Shade" at http://www.fs.fed.us/psw/programs/cufr/). In the Coastal Plain region, there is ample opportunity to "retrofit" communities with more sustainable landscapes through strategic tree planting and care of existing trees.

Retrofit for more savings

Reducing Atmospheric Carbon Dioxide

Global temperatures have increased since the late 19th century, with major warming periods from 1910 to 1945 and from 1976 to the present (IPCC 2001). Human activities, primarily fossil-fuel consumption, are adding greenhouse gases to the atmosphere, and current research suggests that the recent increases in temperature can be attributed in large part to increases in greenhouse gases (IPCC 2001). Higher global temperatures are expected to have a number of adverse effects, including melting polar ice caps which could raise sea level by 6–37 in (15–94 cm) (Hamburg et al. 1997). With most of the Coastal Plain region's population living in coastal areas (Cohen et al. 1997), the effects could be disastrous. Increasing frequency of extreme weather events will continue to tax emergency management resources.

Urban forests have been recognized as important storage sites for carbon dioxide (CO_2), the primary greenhouse gas (Nowak and Crane 2002). Currently, private markets dedicated to reducing CO_2 emissions by trading carbon credits are emerging (McHale 2003; CO2e.com 2005). Carbon credits are selling for up to $20 per **metric tonne** (t), and the social costs of CO_2 emissions are estimated to range from £4 to 27 ($7–47) per t (Pearce 2003). For comparison, for every $19 spent on a tree planting project in Arizona, 1 t of atmospheric CO_2 was reduced (McPherson and Simpson 1999). As carbon trading markets become accredited and prices rise, these markets could provide monetary resources for community forestry programs.

Urban forests can reduce atmospheric CO_2 in two ways (*Figure 5*):

Trees reduce CO_2

- Trees directly sequester CO_2 in their stems and leaves while they grow.
- Trees near buildings can reduce the demand for heating and air conditioning, thereby reducing emissions associated with power production.

17

On the other hand, vehicles, chain saws, chippers, and other equipment release CO_2 during the process of planting and maintaining trees. And eventually, all trees die, and most of the CO_2 that has accumulated in their structure is released into the atmosphere through decomposition. The rate of release into the atmosphere depends on if and how the wood is reused. For instance, recycling of urban wood waste into products such as furniture can delay the rate of decomposition compared to its reuse as mulch.

Typically, CO_2 released due to tree planting, maintenance, and other program-related activities is about 2–8% of annual CO_2 reductions obtained through sequestration and **avoided power plant emissions** (McPherson and Simpson 1999). To provide a complete picture of atmospheric CO_2 reductions from tree plantings, it is important to consider CO_2 released into the atmosphere through tree planting and care activities, as well as decomposition of wood from pruned or dead trees.

Figure 5. Trees sequester CO_2 as they grow and indirectly reduce CO_2 emissions from power plants through energy conservation. At the same time, CO_2 is released through decomposition and tree care activities that involve fossil-fuel consumption (drawing by Mike Thomas).

Avoided CO_2 emissions

Regional variations in climate and the mix of fuels that produce energy to heat and cool buildings influence potential CO_2 emission reductions. Charleston, SC's average emission rate is 1,368 lbs (621 kg) CO_2/kWh (US EPA 2003). Due to the large amount of coal (67%) in the mix of fuels used to generate the power, this emission rate is higher than in some other regions. For example, the two-state average for Oregon and Washington is much lower, 308 lbs (140 kg) CO_2/kWh, because hydroelectric power predominates there. The Coastal Plain region's relatively high CO_2 emission rate means greater benefits from reduced energy demand relative to other regions with lower emissions rates.

CO_2 reduction through community forestry

A study of Houston's regional forest found that the region's 663 million trees store about 39 million tons (35 million t) of atmospheric CO_2 (Smith et al. 2005). These trees sequester approximately 1.6 million tons (1.45 million t) of atmospheric CO_2 annually. The urban forest of Jacksonville, FL, covers about 32% of 125,000 acres and stores a total of about 1.7 million tons (1.5 million t) of CO_2 and sequesters an additional 13,400 tons (12,150 t) each year (American Forests 2005).

Another study in Chicago focused on the carbon sequestration benefit of residential tree **canopy cover**. Tree canopy cover in two residential neighborhoods was estimated to sequester on average 0.112 lb/ft^2 (0.547 kg/m^2), and pruning activities released 0.016 lb/ft^2 (0.08 kg/m^2) (Jo and McPherson 1995). Net annual carbon uptake was 0.096 lb/ft^2 (0.47 kg/m^2).

Since 1990, Trees Forever, an Iowa-based non-profit organization, has planted trees for energy savings and atmospheric CO_2 reduction with utility sponsorships. Over 1 million trees have been planted in 400 communities with the help of 120,000 volunteers. These trees are estimated to offset CO_2 emissions by 50,000 tons (45,359 t) annually. Based on an Iowa State University study, survival rates are an amazing 91% indicating a highly trained and committed volunteer force (Ramsay 2002).

Improving Air Quality

Approximately 159 million people live in areas where **ozone** (O_3) concentrations violate federal air quality standards. About 100 million people live in areas where dust and other small particle matter exceed levels for healthy air. Air pollution is a serious health threat to many city dwellers, causing asthma, coughing, headaches, respiratory and heart disease, and cancer (Smith 1990). Impaired health results in increased social costs for medical care, greater absenteeism, and reduced longevity.

Several areas in the Coastal Plain region (US EPA 2005) do not meet US EPA standards for ozone levels, including the Houston and Baton Rouge metro areas.

Recently, the Environmental Protection Agency (EPA) recognized tree planting as a measure for reducing O_3 in State Implementation Plans. Air quality management districts have funded tree planting projects to control particulate matter. These policy decisions are creating new opportunities to plant and care for trees as a method for controlling air pollution (Luley and Bond 2002, for more information see www.treescleanair.org and our research summary *Trees – The Air Pollution Solution* available at http://www.fs.fed.us/psw/programs/cufr/).

Urban forests provide five main air quality benefits (*Figure 6*):

- They absorb gaseous pollutants (e.g., ozone, **nitrogen dioxide [NO$_2$]**, and **sulfur dioxide [SO$_2$]**) through leaf surfaces.

The EPA recognizes that trees improve air quality

- They intercept small particulate matter (PM_{10}) (e.g., dust, ash, pollen, smoke).

- They release oxygen through **photosynthesis**.

- They transpire water and shade surfaces, which lowers air temperatures, thereby reducing ozone levels.

- They reduce energy use, which reduces emissions of pollutants from power plants, including NO_2, SO_2 PM_{10}, and volatile organic compounds (**VOC**s).

Trees may also adversely affect air quality. Most trees emit **biogenic volatile organic compounds** (BVOCs) such as isoprenes and monoterpenes that can contribute to O_3 formation. The contribution of BVOC emissions from city trees to O_3 formation depends on complex geographic and atmospheric interactions that have not been studied in most cities. Some complicating factors include variations with temperature and atmospheric levels of NO_2. As well, the ozone-forming potential of different tree species varies considerably (Benjamin and Winer 1998). Genera emitting the greatest relative amount of BVOCs are sweetgum (*Liquidambar* spp.), blackgum (*Nyssa* spp.), sycamore (*Platanus* spp.), poplar (*Populus* spp.), and oak (*Quercus* spp.) (Nowak 2000).

A computer simulation study for Atlanta suggested that it would be very difficult to meet EPA ozone standards in the region using trees because of the high BVOC emissions from native pines and other vegetation (Chameides et al. 1988). Although removing trees reduced BVOC emissions, this effect was overwhelmed by increased hydrocarbon emissions from natural and anthropogenic sources due to the increased air temperatures associated with tree removal (Cardelino and Chameides 1990). A similar finding was reported for the Houston-Galveston Area, where deforestation associated with urbanization from 1992–2000 increased surface temperatures. Despite the decrease in BVOC emissions, ozone concentrations increased due to the enhanced urban heat island effect during simulated episodes (Kim et al. 2005). In another study in the Los Angeles basin, increased

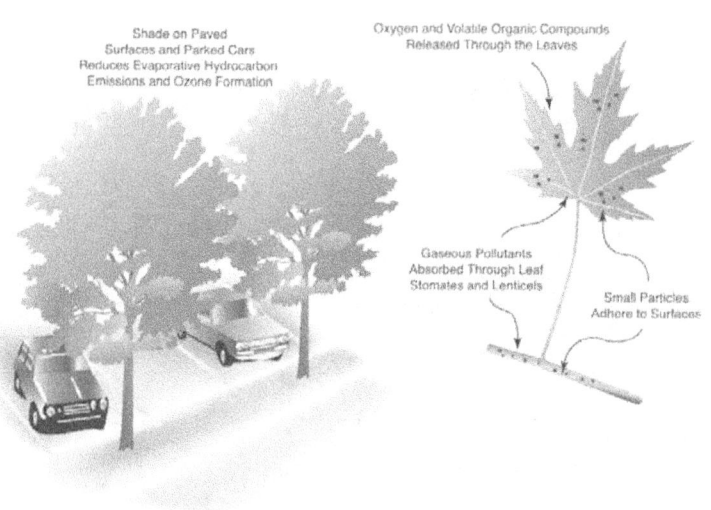

Figure 6. Trees absorb gaseous pollutants, retain particles on their surfaces, and release oxygen and volatile organic compounds. By cooling urban heat islands and shading parked cars, trees can reduce ozone formation (drawing by Mike Thomas).

planting of low BVOC-emitting tree species would reduce O_3 concentrations, while planting of medium- and high-emitters would increase overall O_3 concentrations (Taha 1996). A study in the northeastern United States, however, found that species mix had no detectable effects on O_3 concentrations (Nowak et al. 2000). Any potentially negative effects of trees on one kind of air pollution must be considered in light of their great benefit in other areas such as absorption of other pollutants.

Trees absorb gaseous pollutants through leaf stomates—tiny openings in the leaves. Secondary methods of pollutant removal include adsorption of gases to plant surfaces and uptake through bark pores. Once gases enter the leaf they diffuse into intercellular spaces, where some react with inner leaf surfaces and others are absorbed by water films to form acids. Pollutants can damage plants by altering their metabolism and growth. At high concentrations, pollutants cause visible damage to leaves, such as stippling and bleaching (Costello and Jones 2003). Though they may pose health hazards to plants, pollutants such as nitrogenous gases can also be sources of essential nutrients for trees.

Trees absorb gaseous pollutants

Trees intercept small airborne particles. Some particles that impact a tree are absorbed, but most adhere to plant surfaces. Species with hairy or rough leaf, twig, and bark surfaces are efficient interceptors (Smith and Dochinger 1976). Intercepted particles are often resuspended to the atmosphere when wind blows the branches, and rain will wash some particulates off plant surfaces. The ultimate fate of these pollutants depends on whether they fall onto paved surfaces and enter the stormwater system, or fall on pervious surfaces, where they are filtered in the soil.

Trees intercept particulate matter

Urban forests freshen the air we breathe by releasing oxygen as a by-product of photosynthesis. Net annual oxygen production varies depending on tree species, size, health, and location. A healthy tree, for example a 32-ft tall (10 m) ash, produces about 260 lb (115 kg) of net oxygen annually (McPherson 1997). A typical person consumes 386 lb (175 kg) of oxygen per year. Therefore, two medium-sized, healthy trees can supply the oxygen required for a single person over the course of a year.

Trees release oxygen

Trees near buildings can reduce the demand for heating and air conditioning, thereby reducing emissions of PM_{10}, SO_2, NO_2, and VOCs associated with electric power production. Avoided emissions from trees can be sizable. For example, a strategically located tree can save 100 kWh in electricity for cooling annually (McPherson and Simpson 1999, 2002, 2003). Assuming that this conserved electricity comes from a typical new coal-fired power plant in the Coastal Plain,

Trees save energy, thereby reducing air pollution from power plants

the tree reduces emissions of SO_2 by 1.25 lb (0.57 kg), NO_2 by 0.39 lb (0.18 kg), (US EPA 2003) and PM_{10} by 0.84 lb (0.38 kg) (US EPA 1998). The same tree is responsible for conserving 60 gal (0.23 m³) of water in cooling towers and reducing CO_2 emissions by 200 lb (91 kg).

Trees effectively reduce ozone and particulate matter concentrations

In Houston, TX the tree **canopy** was estimated to remove 60,575 tons (5,590 t) of air pollutants annually with a value of nearly $300 million (Smith et al. 2005). The city of Montgomery, AL's urban forest (33% tree cover) removed 1,603 tons (1,454 t) of air pollutants valued at $7.9 million (American Forests 2004). Chicago's 50.8 million trees were estimated to remove 234 tons (212 t) of PM_{10}, 210 tons (191 t) of O_3, 93 tons (84 t) of sulfur dioxide (SO_2), and 17 tons (15 t) of carbon monoxide in 1991. This environmental service was valued at $9.2 million (Nowak 1994).

What about hydrocarbons?

Trees in a Davis, CA, parking lot were found to improve air quality by reducing air temperatures 1–3°F (0.5–1.5°C) (Scott et al. 1999). By shading asphalt surfaces and parked vehicles, trees reduce hydrocarbon emissions (VOCs) from gasoline that evaporates out of leaky fuel tanks and worn hoses (*Figure 7*; for more information, see our research summary *Where Are All the Cool Parking Lots?* at http://www.fs.fed.us/psw/programs/cufr/). These evaporative emissions are a principal component of smog, and parked vehicles are a primary source. In California, parking lot tree plantings can be funded as an air quality improvement measure because of the associated reductions in evaporative emissions.

Figure 7. Trees planted to shade parking areas can reduce hydrocarbon emissions and improve air quality.

Reducing Stormwater Runoff and Improving Hydrology

Urban stormwater runoff is a major source of pollution entering wetlands, streams, lakes, and oceans. Healthy trees can reduce the amount of runoff and pollutants in receiving waters (Cappiella et al. 2005). This is important because federal law requires states and localities to control nonpoint-source pollution, such as runoff from pavements, buildings, and landscapes. Trees are mini-reservoirs, controlling runoff at the source, thereby reducing runoff volumes and erosion of watercourses, as well as delaying the onset of **peak flows**. Trees can reduce runoff in several ways (*Figure 8*; for more information, see "Is All Your Rain Going Down the Drain?" at http://www.fs.fed.us/psw/programs/cufr/):

- Leaves and branch surfaces intercept and store rainfall, thereby reducing runoff volumes and delaying the onset of peak flows.

- Roots increase the rate at which rainfall infiltrates soil and the capacity of soil to store water, reducing overland flow.

- Tree canopies reduce soil erosion by diminishing the impact of raindrops on barren surfaces.

- **Transpiration** through tree leaves reduces soil moisture, increasing the soil's capacity to store rainfall.

Rainfall that is stored temporarily on canopy leaf and bark surfaces is called intercepted rainfall. Intercepted water evaporates, drips from leaf surfaces, and flows down stem surfaces to the ground. **Tree-surface saturation** generally occurs after 1–2 inches (2.5–5 cm) of rainfall has fallen (Xiao et al. 2000). During large storm events, rainfall exceeds the amount that the tree **crown** can store, about 50–100 gal (0.19–

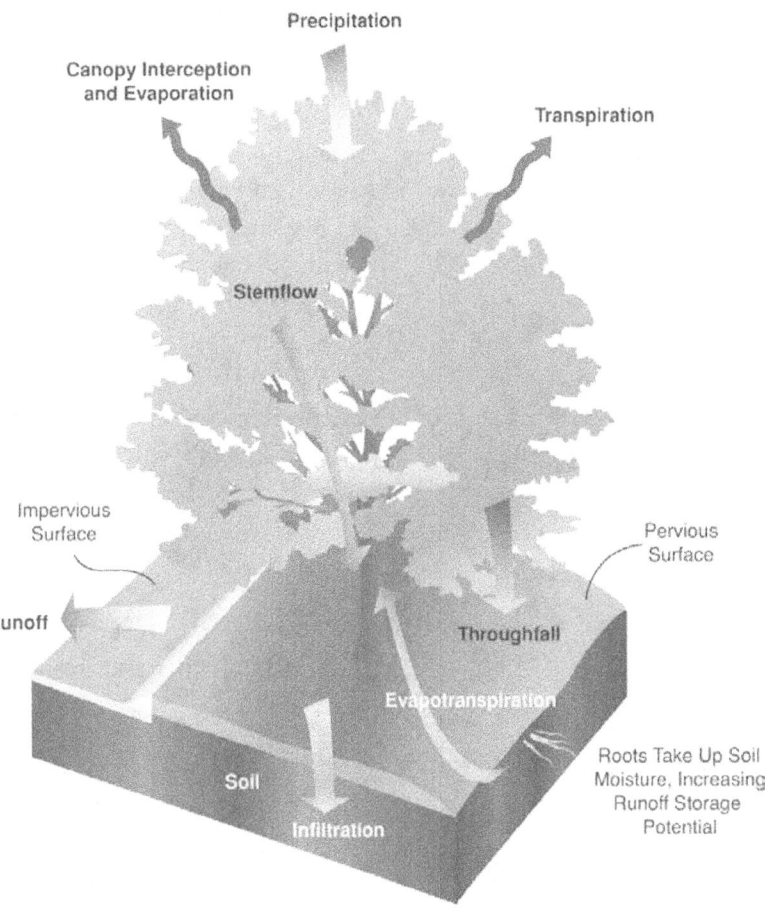

Figure 8. Trees intercept a portion of rainfall that evaporates and never reaches the ground. Some rainfall runs to the ground along branches and stems (stemflow) and some falls through gaps or drips off leaves and branches (throughfall). Transpiration increases soil moisture storage potential (drawing by Mike Thomas).

23

0.38 m³) per tree. The **interception** benefit is the amount of rainfall that does not reach the ground because it evaporates from the crown. As a result, the volume of runoff is reduced and the time of peak flow is delayed. Trees protect water quality by substantially reducing runoff during small rainfall events that are responsible for most pollutant washoff. Therefore, urban forests generally produce more benefits through water quality protection than through flood control (Xiao et al 1998, 2000).

The amount of rainfall trees intercept depends on their architecture, rainfall patterns, and climate. Tree-crown characteristics that influence interception are the trunk, stem, and surface areas, textures, area of gaps, period when leaves are present, and dimensions (e.g., **tree height** and diameter). Trees with coarse surfaces retain more rainfall than those with smooth surfaces. Large trees generally intercept more rainfall than small trees do because greater surface areas allow for greater evaporation rates. Tree crowns with few gaps reduce **throughfall** to the ground. Species that are in-leaf when rainfall is plentiful are more effective than deciduous species that have dropped their leaves during the rainy season.

Value of runoff reduction

Studies that have simulated urban forest effects on stormwater runoff have reported reductions of 2–7%. Annual interception of rainfall by Sacramento's urban forest for the total urbanized area was only about 2% due to the winter rainfall pattern and lack of **evergreen** species (Xiao et al. 1998). However, average interception under the tree canopy ranged from 6 to 13% (150 gal [0.57 m³] per tree), close to values reported for rural forests. Broadleaf evergreens and **conifers** intercept more rainfall than deciduous species in areas where rainfall is highest in fall, winter, or spring (Xiao and McPherson 2002).

The city of Montgomery, Alabama's tree canopy (34%) reduced runoff by 227 million cubic feet (6.5 million m³), valued at $454 million per 20-year construction cycle (American Forests 2004). In Charlotte, NC, the existing street tree canopy reduced runoff by 28 million cubic feet (793,000 m³), with an estimated value of $2 million (McPherson et al. 2005b).

Urban forests can treat wastewater

Urban forests can provide other hydrologic benefits, too. For example, tree plantations or nurseries can be irrigated with partially treated wastewater. Infiltration of water through the soil can be a safe and productive means of water treatment. Reused wastewater applied to urban forest lands can recharge aquifers, reduce stormwater-treatment loads, and create income through sales of nursery or wood products. Recycling urban wastewater into greenspace areas can be an economical means of treatment and disposal, while at the same time providing other environmental benefits (NRCS 2005).

Aesthetics and Other Benefits

Trees provide a host of aesthetic, social, economic, and health benefits that should be included in any benefit–cost analysis. One of the most frequently cited reasons that people plant trees is for beautification. Trees add color, texture, line, and form to the landscape. In this way, trees soften the hard geometry that dominates built environments. Research on the aesthetic quality of residential streets has shown that street trees are the single strongest positive influence on scenic quality (Schroeder and Cannon 1983).

Figure 9. Trees beautify a neighborhood, increasing property values and creating a more sociable environment.

Consumer surveys have found that preference ratings increase with the presence of trees in the commercial streetscape. In contrast to areas without trees, shoppers shop more often and longer in well-landscaped business districts. They are willing to pay more for parking and up to 11% more for goods and services (Wolf 1999).

Attractiveness of retail settings

Research in public housing complexes found that outdoor spaces with trees were used significantly more often than spaces without trees. By facilitating interactions among residents, trees can contribute to reduced levels of domestic violence, as well as foster safer and more sociable neighborhood environments (Sullivan and Kuo 1996).

Public safety benefits

Well-maintained trees increase the "curb appeal" of properties (*Figure 9*). Research comparing sales prices of residential properties with different numbers of trees suggests that people are willing to pay 3–7% more for properties with ample trees versus few or no trees. One of the most comprehensive studies of the influence of trees on home property values was based on actual sales prices and found that each large front-yard tree was associated with about a 1% increase in sales price (Anderson and Cordell 1988). A much greater value of 9% ($15,000) was determined in a U.S. Tax Court case for the loss of a large black oak on a property valued at $164,500 (Neely 1988). Depending on average home sales prices, the value of this benefit can contribute significantly to cities' property tax revenues.

Property value benefits

Scientific studies confirm our intuition that trees in cities provide social and psychological benefits. Humans derive substantial plea-

Social and psychological benefits

sure from trees, whether it is inspiration from their beauty, a spiritual connection, or a sense of meaning (Dwyer et al. 1992; Lewis 1996). Following natural disasters people often report a sense of loss if their community forest has been damaged (Hull 1992). Views of trees and nature from homes and offices provide restorative experiences that ease mental fatigue and help people to concentrate (Kaplan and Kaplan 1989). Desk-workers with a view of nature report lower rates of sickness and greater satisfaction with their jobs compared to those having no visual connection to nature (Kaplan 1992). Trees provide important settings for recreation and relaxation in and near cities. The act of planting trees can have social value, as bonds between people and local groups often result.

Human health benefits

The presence of trees in cities provides public health benefits and improves the well-being of those who live, work, and play in cities. Physical and emotional stress has both short-term and long-term effects. Prolonged stress can compromise the human immune system. A series of studies on human stress caused by general urban conditions and city driving show that views of nature reduce stress response of both body and mind (Parsons et al. 1998). Urban green also appears to have an "immunization effect," in that people show less stress response if they have had a recent view of trees and vegetation. Hospitalized patients with views of nature and time spent outdoors need less medication, sleep better, have a better outlook, and recover more quickly than patients without connections to nature (Ulrich 1985). Skin cancer is a particular concern in the sunny Coastal Plain region. Trees reduce exposure to ultraviolet light, thereby lowering the risk of harmful effects from skin cancer and cataracts (Tretheway and Manthe 1999).

Certain environmental benefits from trees are more difficult to quantify than those previously described, but can be just as important. Noise can reach unhealthy levels in cities. Trucks, trains, and planes can produce noise that exceeds 100 decibels, twice the level at which noise becomes a health risk. Thick strips of vegetation in conjunction with landforms or solid barriers can reduce highway noise by 6–15 decibels. Plants absorb more high frequency noise than low frequency, which is advantageous to humans since higher frequencies are most distressing to people (Cook 1978).

Figure 10. Natural areas within cities are refuges for wildlife and help connect city dwellers with their ecosystems.

Numerous types of wildlife inhabit cities and are generally highly valued by residents. For example, older parks, cemeteries, and botanical gardens often contain a rich assemblage of wildlife. Remnant woodlands and **riparian habitats** within cities can connect a city to its surrounding bioregion (*Figure 10*). Wetlands, greenways (linear parks), and other greenspace can provide habitats that conserve **biodiversity** (Platt et al. 1994).

Wildlife habitat

Urban forestry can provide jobs for both skilled and unskilled labor. Public service programs and grassroots-led urban and community forestry programs provide horticultural training to volunteers across the United States. Also, urban and community forestry provides educational opportunities for residents who want to learn about nature through first-hand experience (McPherson and Mathis 1999). Local nonprofit tree groups and municipal volunteer programs often provide educational material and hands-on training in the care of trees and work with area schools.

Jobs and environmental education

Tree shade on streets can help offset pavement management costs by protecting paving from weathering. The asphalt paving on streets contains stone aggregate in an oil binder. Tree shade lowers the street surface temperature and reduces heating and volatilization of the binder (McPherson and Muchnick 2005). As a result, the aggregate remains protected for a longer period by the oil binder. When unprotected, vehicles loosen the aggregate, and much like sandpaper, the loose aggregate grinds down the pavement. Because most weathering of asphalt-concrete pavement occurs during the first 5 to 10 years, when new street tree plantings provide little shade, this benefit mainly applies when older streets are resurfaced (*Figure 11*).

Shade can reduce street maintenance

Figure 11. Although shade trees can be expensive to maintain, their shade can reduce the costs of resurfacing streets (McPherson and Muchnick 2005), promote pedestrian travel, and improve air quality directly through pollutant uptake and indirectly through reduced emissions of volatile organic compounds from cars.

27

Costs

Cities in the Coastal Plain spend about $18 per tree

The environmental, social, and economic benefits of urban and community forests come, of course, at a price. Our survey of **municipal foresters** in Jacksonville, FL, Savannah, GA, and Charleston, SC, indicates that they are spending about $18 per tree annually. Most of this amount is for pruning ($8 per tree), planting ($4 per tree), removal and disposal ($2 per tree) and administration ($2 per tree). Other municipal departments incur costs for infrastructure repair that average about $2 per tree annually.

Residential levels of service and costs vary

Annual expenditures for tree management on private property have not been well documented. Costs vary considerably, ranging from some commercial or residential properties that receive regular professional landscape service to others that are virtually "wild" and without maintenance. Our survey of commercial arborists in the Coastal Plain indicated that expenditures typically range from $12 to $18 per tree. Expenditures are usually greatest for pruning, planting, and removal.

Planting and Maintaining Trees

Tree planting and pruning

Planting costs include the cost of the tree and the cost for planting, staking, and mulching. Based on our survey of Coastal Plain municipal and commercial arborists, planting costs vary with tree size and range from $150 for a 15-gallon tree to $550 for a 4-in tree. Pruning cycles vary by city and by tree size and range from once in four years for new trees to once in ten years for large, mature trees. The cost for pruning young trees ranged from $25 for a public tree to $45 for a yard tree; the cost to prune a large, mature tree ranged from approximately $275 for public trees to $500 for yard trees. Conifers have substantially lower pruning costs, especially in the Coastal Plain region, where many conifers are self-pruning.

Irrigation costs

Due to the region's warm summer climate, newly planted trees may require watering for a couple of years. Once established, trees in the Coastal Plain rarely require additional irrigation. During drought years, however, a small annual cost may occur.

Tree and stump removal costs

At the end of a tree's life, removal costs can be substantial, especially for large trees. Removal and disposal of small trees (under 3 inches in DBH [7.6 cm]) costs less than $40, but a large tree may cost several thousand dollars to remove. According to our survey, total costs for removal of trees and stumps average approximately $40 per inch ($15.75 per cm) DBH for yard trees and $25 per inch ($9.84 cm) DBH for public trees.

Conflicts with Urban Infrastructure

Like other cities across the United States, communities in the Coastal Plain region are spending millions of dollars each year to manage conflicts between trees and powerlines, sidewalks, sewers, and other elements of the urban infrastructure. According to the city forester of Charleston, SC, Charleston spends an average of $60,000 or about $2 per tree on sidewalk, curb, and gutter repair costs. This amount is far less than the $11.22 per tree reported for 18 California cities (McPherson 2000) and less than one-third the amount that the city of Charlotte, NC, reported in an earlier survey (McPherson et al. 2005b). In addition, the figures for California apply only to street trees and do not include repair costs for damaged sewer lines, building foundations, parking lots, and various other **hardscape** elements.

In some cities, decreasing budgets are increasing the sidewalk-repair backlog and forcing cities to shift the costs of sidewalk repair to residents. This shift has significant impacts on residents in older areas, where large trees have outgrown small sites and infrastructure has deteriorated. It should be noted that trees should not always bear full reponsibility. In older areas, in particular, sidewalks and curbs may have reached the end of their 20–25 year service life, or may have been poorly constructed in the first place (Sydnor et al. 2000).

Efforts to control the costs of these conflicts are having alarming effects on urban forests (Bernhardt and Swiecki 1993, Thompson and Ahern 2000):

- Cities are downsizing their urban forests by planting smaller trees. Although small trees are appropriate under power lines and in small planting sites, they are less effective than large trees at providing shade, absorbing air pollutants, and intercepting rainfall.

- Sidewalk damage was the second most common reason that street and park trees were removed. Thousands of healthy urban trees are lost each year and their benefits forgone because of this problem.

- Most cities surveyed were removing more trees than they were planting. Residents forced to pay for sidewalk repairs may not want replacement trees.

Cost-effective strategies to retain benefits from large street trees while reducing costs associated with infrastructure conflicts are described in *Strategies to Reduce Infrastructure Damage by Tree Roots* (Costello and Jones 2003). Matching the growth characteristics of trees to the conditions at the planting site is one important strategy.

Tree roots can damage sidewalks

Cost of conflicts

Trees and conflicts with sewer lines

Tree roots can also damage old sewer lines that are cracked or otherwise susceptible to invasion. Sewer repair companies estimate that sewer damage is minor until trees and sewers are over 30 years old, and roots from trees in yards are usually more of a problem than roots from trees in planter strips along streets. The latter assertion may be due to the fact that sewers are closer to the root zone as they enter houses than at the street. Repair costs typically range from $100 for sewer roding (inserting a cleaning implement to temporarily remove roots) to $1,000 or more for sewer excavation and replacement.

Cleaning up after trees

Most communities sweep their streets regularly to reduce surface-runoff pollution entering local waterways. Street trees drop leaves, flowers, fruit, and branches year round that constitute a significant portion of debris collected from city streets. When leaves fall and rains begin, **tree litter** can clog sewers, dry wells, and other elements of flood-control systems. Costs include additional labor needed to remove leaves, and property damage caused by localized flooding. Windstorms also incur clean-up costs. Serious natural catastrophes are more frequent in the Coastal Plain region than they are in other areas and can result in large expenditures.

The cost of addressing conflicts between trees and power lines is reflected in electric rates. Large trees under power lines require more frequent pruning than better-suited trees, which can make them appear less attractive (*Figure 12*). Frequent crown reduction reduces the benefits these trees could otherwise provide. Moreover, increased costs for pruning are passed on to customers.

Figure 12. Large trees planted under power lines can require extensive pruning, which increases tree care costs and reduces the benefits of those trees, including their appearance.

Chapter 3. Determining Benefits and Costs of Community Forests in Coastal Plain Communities

This chapter presents estimated benefits and costs for trees planted in typical residential yards and public sites. Because benefits and costs vary with tree size, we report results for representative **large**, **medium**, and **small** broadleaf **trees** and for a representative conifer.

Estimates are initial approximations as some benefits and costs are intangible or difficult to quantify (e.g., impacts on psychological health, crime, and violence). Limited knowledge about physical processes at work and their interactions makes estimates imprecise (e.g., fate of air pollutants trapped by trees and then washed to the ground by rainfall). Tree growth and mortality rates are highly variable throughout the region. Benefits and costs also vary, depending on differences in climate, pollutant concentrations, maintenance practices, and other factors. Given the Coastal Plain region's broad area, with many different climates, soils, and types of community forestry programs, the approach used here provides first-order approximations. It is a general accounting that can be easily adapted and adjusted for local planting projects. It provides a basis for decisions that set priorities and influence management direction (Maco and McPherson 2003).

Figure 13. The flowering dogwood represents small trees in this guide.

Overview of Procedures

Approach

In this study, annual benefits and costs are estimated over a 40-year planning horizon for newly planted trees in three residential yard locations (east, south, and west of the residence) and a public streetside or park location (*Appendix B*). Henceforth, we refer to trees in these hypothetical locations as "yard" trees and "public" trees, respectively. Prices are assigned to each cost (e.g., planting, pruning, removal, irrigation, infrastructure repair, liability) and benefit (e.g., heating/cooling energy savings, air pollutant mitigation, stormwater runoff reduction, aesthetic and other benefits measured as increases in property value) through direct estimation and implied valuation of benefits as environmental externalities. This approach makes it possible to estimate the net benefits of plantings in "typical" locations using "typical" tree species. More information on data collection, modeling procedures, and assumptions can be found in *Appendix C*.

To account for differences in the mature size and growth of different tree species, we report results for a large (*Quercus virginiana*, Southern live oak), medium (*Magnolia grandiflora*, Southern magnolia), and small (*Cornus florida*, dogwood) broadleaf tree and a conifer (*Pinus taeda*, loblolly pine) (*Figures 13–16*). Tree dimensions are

Benefit and cost estimation

Figure 14. The Southern magnolia represents medium trees in this guide.

31

Figure 15. The Southern live oak represents large trees in this guide.

Tree benefits based on numerical models

Tree mortality included

Figure 16. The loblolly pine represents coniferous trees in this guide.

derived from growth curves developed from street trees in Charleston, SC (McPherson et al. 2006a) (*Figure 17*).

Frequency and costs of tree management are estimated based on surveys with municipal foresters from Jacksonville, FL, Savannah, GA, and Charleston, SC. In addition, commercial arborists from Summerville, SC, Houston, TX, and Athens, GA, provided information on tree-management costs on residential properties.

Benefits are calculated with numerical models and data both from the region (e.g., pollutant emission factors factors for avoided emissions due to energy savings) and from local sources (e.g., Charleston climate data for energy effects). Regional electricity and natural gas prices are used in this study to quantify energy savings. Damage and control costs are used to estimate **willingness to pay.** For example, the value of stormwater runoff reduction due to rainfall interception by trees is estimated using marginal control costs. If a community or developer is willing to pay an average of $0.01 per gal of treated and controlled runoff to meet minimum standards, then the stormwater runoff mitigation value of a tree that intercepts 1,000 gal of rainfall, eliminating the need for control, should be $10.

Reporting Results

Results are reported in terms of annual value per tree planted. To make these calculations realistic, however, mortality rates are included. Based on our survey of regional municipal foresters and commercial arborists, this analysis assumes that 35% of the planted trees will die over the 40-year period. Annual mortality rates are 1.5% per year for the first 5 years and 0.8% per year for the remainder of the 40-year period. This accounting approach "grows" trees in different locations and uses computer simulation to directly calculate the annual flow of benefits and costs as trees mature and die (McPherson 1992). In *Appendix B*, results are reported at 5-year intervals for 40 years.

Findings of This Study

Average Annual Net Benefits

Average annual net benefits (benefits minus costs) per tree over a 40-year period increase with mature tree size (for detailed results see *Appendix B*):

- $87 to $108 for a large tree

- $16 to $26 for a medium tree

- $1 to $7 for a small tree

- $40 to $51 for a conifer

Our findings demonstrate that average annual net benefits from large trees, like the live oak, are substantially greater than those from small trees like dogwood. Average annual net benefits for the small, medium, and large broadleaf public trees are $1, $19, and $97, respectively. Conifers provide an intermediate level of benefits, on average $41 for a public tree. The largest average annual net benefits, however, stemmed from yard trees opposite the west-facing wall of a house: $7, $26, $108, and $51, for small, medium, and large broadleaf trees and the conifer, respectively.

At year 40, the large yard tree opposite a west or east wall produces a net annual benefit of $169. In the same location, 40 years after planting, the magnolia, dogwood and loblolly pine produce annual net benefits of $41, $15 and $87.

Forty years after planting at a typical public site, the large, medium, and small broadleaf trees and the conifer provide annual net benefits of $158, $27, $8, and $74, respectively.

Net benefits for a yard tree opposite a west or east house wall and a public tree also increase with size when summed over the entire 40-year period:

- $4,320 (yard) and $3,880 (public) for a large tree

- $1,040 (yard) and $760 (public) for a medium tree

- $280 (yard) and $40 (public) for a small tree

- $2,040 (yard) and $1,640 (public) for a conifer

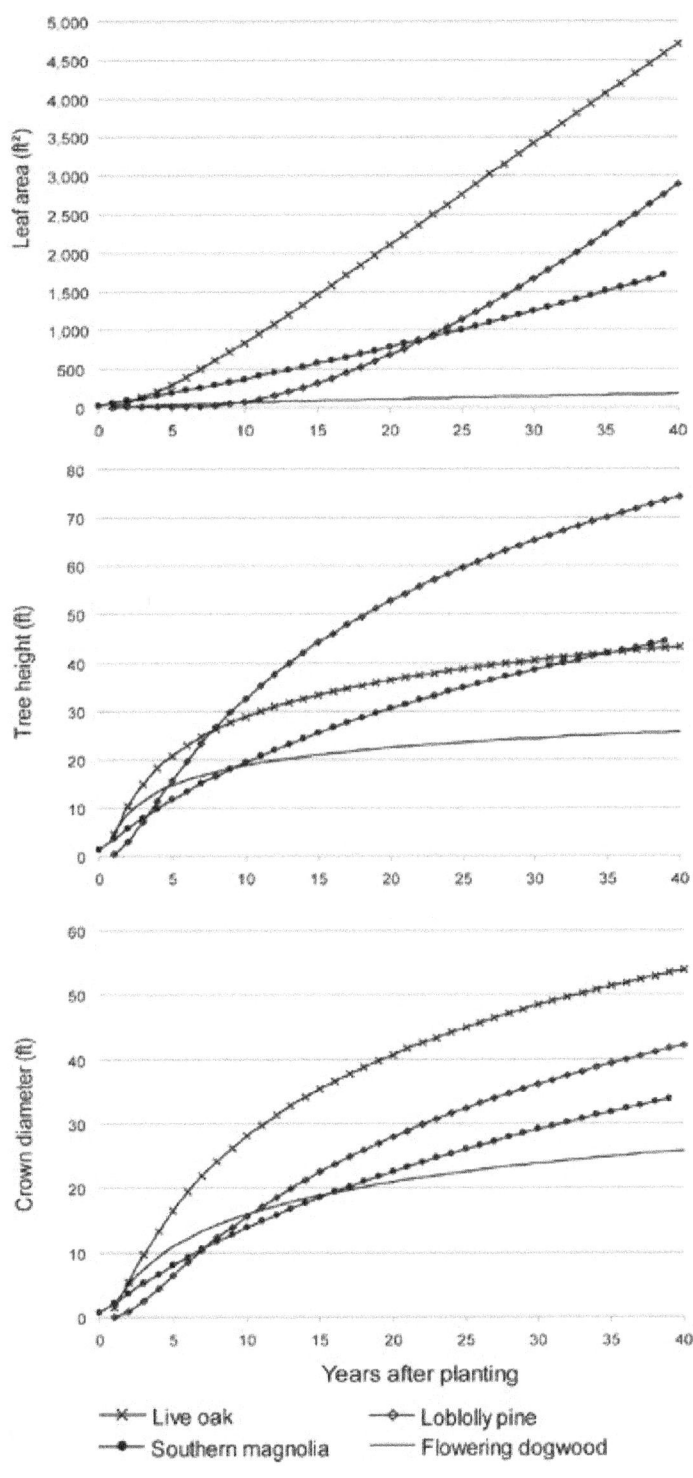

Figure 17. Tree growth curves are based on data collected from street trees in Charleston, SC. Data for representative large, medium, small and conifer trees are for the live oak, Southern magnolia, flowering dogwood, and loblolly pine, respectively. Differences in leaf surface area among species are most important for this analysis because functional benefits such as summer shade, rainfall interception, and pollutant uptake are related to leaf area.

33

Table 1. Estimated annual benefits and costs for a yard tree opposite a west-facing wall 20 years after planting.

Benefit category	Flowering dogwood Small tree 23 ft tall 22 ft spread Leaf surface area = 112 ft²			Southern magnolia Medium tree 29 ft tall 22 ft spread Leaf surface area = 739 ft²			Live oak Large tree 36 ft tall 41 ft spread Leaf surface area = 2,102 ft²			Loblolly pine Conifer tree 53 ft tall 28 ft spread Leaf surface area = 681 ft²		
	RUs		Total $	RUs		Total $	RUs		Total $	RUs		Total $
Electricity savings ($0 0934/kWh)	100	kWh	9 34	135	kWh	12 59	386	kWh	36 01	213	kWh	19 92
Natural gas savings ($0 0120/kBtu)	104	kBtu	1 25	-29	kBtu	-0 34	127	kBtu	1 52	103	kBtu	1 23
Carbon dioxide ($0 0075/lb)	170	lb	1 28	217	lb	1 63	733	lb	5 50	382	lb	2 87
Ozone ($1 04/lb)	0 17	lb	0 18	0 24	lb	0 25	0 84	lb	0 88	0 40	lb	0 41
NO₂ ($1 04/lb)	0 24	lb	0 25	0 31	lb	0 32	0 98	lb	1 02	0 51	lb	0 53
SO₂ ($1 28/lb)	0 69	lb	0 88	0 89	lb	1 15	2 72	lb	3 49	1 43	lb	1 84
PM₁₀ ($0 76/lb)	0 17	lb	0 13	0 25	lb	0 19	0 52	lb	0 39	0 32	lb	0 24
VOCs ($1 48/lb)	0 05	lb	0 08	0 07	lb	0 10	0 21	lb	0 31	0 11	lb	0 16
BVOCs ($1 48/lb)	0 00	lb	0 00	-0 88	lb	-1 30	-1 95	lb	-2 89	-1 50	lb	-2 22
Rainfall interception ($0 006/gal)	720	gal	4 36	1,646	gal	9 96	5,226	gal	31 62	2,098	gal	12 70
Environmental subtotal			**17.79**			**24.55**			**77 85**			**37.69**
Other benefits			1 29			13 80			52 77			26 48
Total benefits			**19.09**			**38.35**			**130.62**			**64.17**
Total costs (see *Table 3*)			**-8.26**			**-9.23**			**-11 93**			**-5.60**
Net benefits			**10.83**			**29.12**			**118.68**			**58.57**

RU Resource unit

Table 2. Estimated annual benefits and costs for a public tree (street/park) 20 years after planting.

Benefit category	Flowering dogwood Small tree 23 ft tall 22 ft spread Leaf surface area = 112 ft²			Southern magnolia Medium tree 29 ft tall 22 ft spread Leaf surface area = 739 ft²			Live oak Large tree 36 ft tall 41 ft spread Leaf surface area = 2,102 ft²			Loblolly pine Conifer tree 52 ft tall 28 ft spread Leaf surface area = 681 ft²		
	RUs		Total $	RUs		Total $	RUs		Total $	RUs		Total $
Electricity savings ($0 0934/kWh)	52	kWh	4 85	55	kWh	5 12	192	kWh	17 95	89	kWh	8 31
Natural gas savings ($0 0120/kBtu)	188	kBtu	2 25	201	kBtu	2 41	563	kBtu	6 74	311	kBtu	3 72
Carbon dioxide ($0 0075/lb)	113	lb	0 85	135	lb	1 01	520	lb	3 90	237	lb	1 78
Ozone ($1 04/lb)	0 17	lb	0 18	0 24	lb	0 25	0 84	lb	0 88	0 40	lb	0 41
NO₂ ($1 04/lb)	0 24	lb	0 25	0 31	lb	0 32	0 98	lb	1 02	0 51	lb	0 53
SO₂ ($1 28/lb)	0 69	lb	0 88	0 89	lb	1 15	2 72	lb	3 49	1 43	lb	1 84
PM₁₀ ($0 76/lb)	0 17	lb	0 13	0 25	lb	0 19	0 52	lb	0 39	0 32	lb	0 24
VOCs ($1 48/lb)	0 05	lb	0 08	0 07	lb	0 10	0 21	lb	0 31	0 11	lb	0 16
BVOCs ($1 48/lb)	0 00	lb	0 00	-0 88	lb	-1 30	-1 95	lb	-2 89	-1 50	lb	-2 22
Rainfall interception ($0 006/gal)	720	gal	4 36	1,646	gal	9 96	5,226	gal	31 62	2,098	gal	12 70
Environmental subtotal			**13 83**			**19.21**			**63.40**			**27.47**
Other benefits			1 44			15 42			58 94			29 57
Total benefits			**15.28**			**34.63**			**122.34**			**57.04**
Total costs (see *Table 3*)			**-10 39**			**-11.69**			**-15.30**			**-10.16**
Net benefits			**4 89**			**22 94**			**107.04**			**46.89**

RU Resource unit

Twenty years after planting, average annual benefits for all trees exceed costs of tree planting and management (*Tables 1* and *2*). For a large live oak in a yard 20 years after planting, the total value of environmental benefits alone ($78) is nearly seven times the total annual cost ($12). Environmental benefits total $25, $18, and $38 for the magnolia, dogwood, and loblolly pine, while tree care costs are similarly lower, $9, $8, and $6, respectively. Adding the value of aesthetics and other benefits to the environmental benefits results in substantial net benefits.

Net benefits are less for public trees (*Table 2*) than yard trees for two main reasons. First, public tree care costs are greater because public trees generally receive more intensive care than private trees. Second, energy benefits are lower for public trees than for yard trees because public trees are assumed to provide general climate effects, but not to shade buildings directly.

Average Annual Costs

Averaged over 40 years, the costs for yard and public trees, respectively, are as follows:

- $19 and $23 for a large tree
- $15 and $18 for a medium tree
- $12 and $14 for a small tree
- $10 and $14 for a conifer

Over the 40-year period, tree pruning is the single greatest cost for public and yard trees (excluding the conifer which requires little pruning), averaging approximately $3 to $10 per tree per year (see *Appendix B*). Annualized expenditures for tree planting are an important

Greatest costs for pruning and planting

Table 3. Estimated annual costs 20 years after planting for a yard tree opposite a west-facing wall and a public tree.

Costs ($/year/tree)	Flowering dogwood Small tree 23 ft tall 22 ft spread Leaf surface area = 112 ft²		Southern magnolia Medium tree 29 ft tall 22 ft spread Leaf surface area = 739 ft²		Live oak Large tree 36 ft tall 41 ft spread Leaf surface area = 2,102 ft²		Loblolly pine Conifer tree 52 ft tall 28 ft spread Leaf surface area = 681 ft²	
	Yard: west	Public tree	Yard: west	Public tree	Yard: west	Public tree	Yard: west	Public tree
Pruning	5 01	6 05	5 01	6 05	5 01	6 05	0 26	3 03
Remove & dispose	2 73	1 70	3 55	2 22	5 82	3 64	4 49	2 81
Pest & disease	0 35	0 00	0 45	0 00	0 74	0 00	0 57	0 00
Infrastructure	0 12	1 16	0 15	1 51	0 25	2 47	0 19	1 91
Clean-up	0 05	0 54	0 07	0 70	0 11	1 15	0 09	0 89
Admin & other	0 00	0 93	0 00	1 21	0 00	1 98	0 00	1 53
Total costs	**8.26**	**10.39**	**9.23**	**11.69**	**11.93**	**15.30**	**5.60**	**10.16**
Total benefits	19 09	15 28	38 35	34 63	130 62	122 34	64 17	57 04
Total net benefits	**10.83**	**4.89**	**29 12**	**22.94**	**118.68**	**107.04**	**58.57**	**46.89**

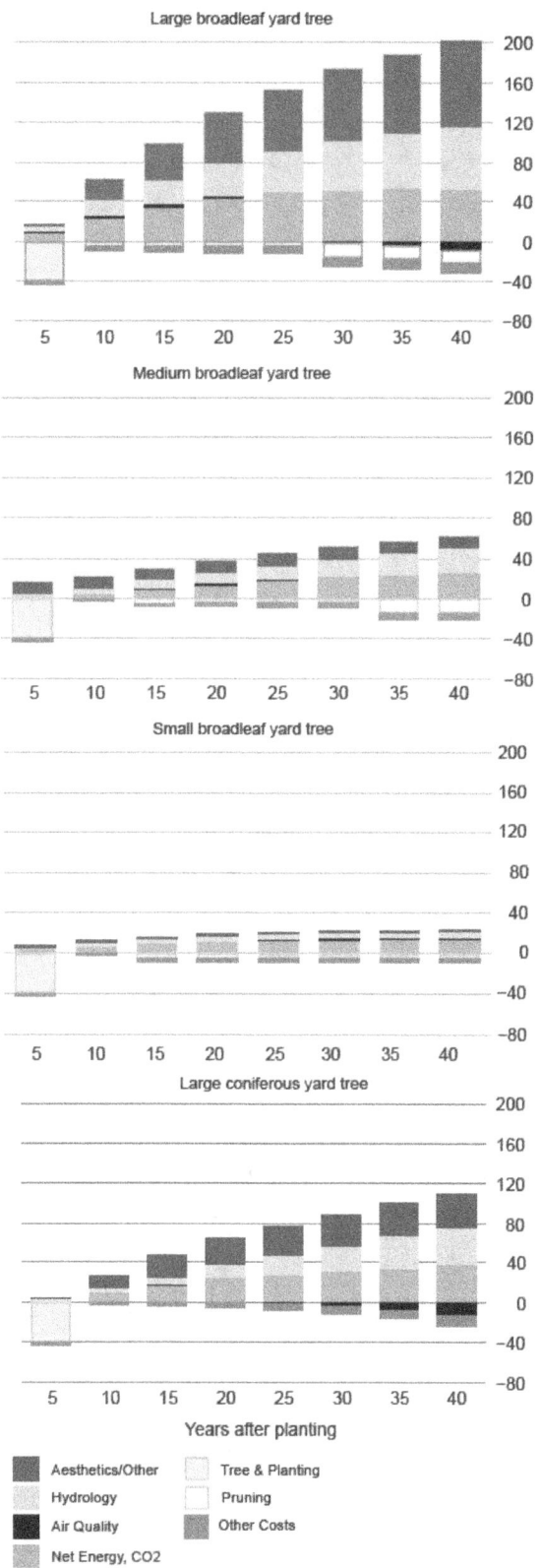

Figure 18. Estimated annual benefits and costs for a large (Southern live oak), medium (Southern magnolia), and small (dogwood) broadleaf tree and a conifer (loblolly pine) located west of a residence.

cost, especially for trees planted in private yards ($5 per tree per year). Based on our survey, we assume in this study that a yard tree with a 2.5-in (6.35-cm) **diameter at breast height** (DBH) is planted at a cost of $200. The cost for planting a 15-gallon public tree is $150.

Table 3 shows annual management costs 20 years after planting for yard trees to the west of a house and for public trees. Annual costs for yard trees range from $6 to $12, while public tree care costs are $10 to $15. In general, public trees are more expensive to maintain than yard trees because of their prominence and because of the greater need for public safety.

Average Annual Benefits

Average annual benefits, including stormwater reduction, aesthetic value, air quality improvement and CO_2 sequestration increase with mature tree size (*Figures 18* and *19*, for detailed results see *Appendix C*):

- $14 to $19 for a small tree
- $31 to $40 for a medium tree
- $107 to $127 for a large tree
- $50 to $62 for a conifer

Stormwater Runoff Reduction

Benefits associated with rainfall interception, reducing stormwater runoff, are substantial for all tree types. The live oak intercepts 5,699 gal/year (21.6 m³/year) on average over a 40-year period with an implied value of $35. The magnolia, dogwood, and loblolly pine intercept 1,962 gal/year (7.4 m³/year), 723 gal/year (2.7 m³/year) and 2,816 gal/year (10.7 m³/year) on average, with values of $12, $4, and $17, respectively.

As the cities of the Coastal Plain continue to grow, the amount of impervious surface will continue to increase dramatically. The role that trees, in combination with other strategies such as rain gardens and structural soils, can play in reducing stormwater runoff is substantial.

Energy Savings

Trees provide significant energy benefits that tend to increase with tree size. For example, average annual net energy benefits over the 40-year period are $10 for the small dogwood opposite a west-facing wall, and $35 for the larger live oak. Average annual net energy benefits for public trees are less than for yard trees because public trees are assumed to provide general climate effects, but not to shade buildings directly. Benefits for public trees range from $7 for the dogwood to $24 for the live oak. For species of all sizes, energy savings increase as trees mature and their leaf surface areas increase (*Figures 18 and 19*).

As expected in a region with hot, humid summers and very mild winters, cooling savings account for most of the total energy benefit. Average annual cooling savings over the 40-year period for the dogwood range from $4 to $9 and heating savings from only $1 to $2. Average annual cooling savings for the live oak range from $16 to $34, but the evergreen live oak may actually have a negative effect on heating costs, depending on planting location. When planted on the east or west sides of a house, the live oak has a small positive average effect on heating costs ($1), but planted on the southern side of a house, it has an average negative effect of $–9, because it blocks the warm southern rays of the winter sun (see also *Figure 4*). The same is true for the magnolia and loblolly pine planted on the southern side ($–4 each).

Average annual net energy benefits for residential trees are similar for a tree located west and east of a building. Cooling savings due to tree shade are comparable for east and west trees, but trees located east of a building slightly increase heating costs due to greater winter shade than do trees to the west. A yard tree located south of a building produces the least net energy benefit because it has the least benefit during summer, and the greatest adverse effect on heating costs from shade in winter. Net energy benefits also reflect species-related traits such as size, form, crown density, and time in leaf.

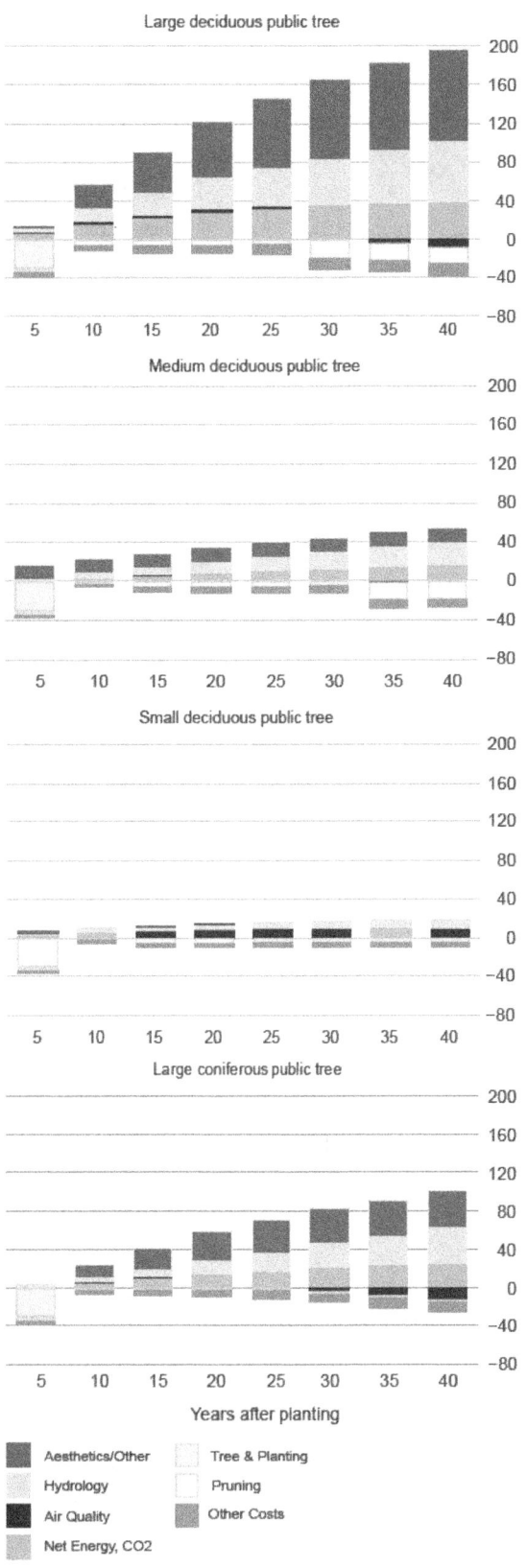

Figure 19. Estimated annual benefits and costs for a large (live oak), medium (Southern magnolia), and small (dogwood) broadleaf tree and a conifer (loblolly pine) public tree.

37

Carbon Dioxide Reduction

All tree types reduce CO₂

Net atmospheric CO_2 reductions accrue for all tree types. Average annual net reductions range from a high of 680 lbs (310 kg) ($5.10) for a large tree on the west or east side of a house to a low of 99 lbs (45 kg) ($0.74) for a small tree on the southern side of the house. Deciduous trees opposite west-facing house walls generally produce the greatest CO_2 reduction due to avoided power plant emissions associated with energy savings. The values for the dogwood are lowest for CO_2 reduction because its very small leaf area and slow growth mean that it is sequestering little CO_2.

Forty years after planting, average annual avoided emissions and sequestered and released CO_2 for a yard tree opposite a west wall are 889 lbs (403 kg), 413 lbs (187 kg), 197 lbs (89 kg) and 618 lbs (280 kg), respectively, for the large, medium, and small broadleaf trees and the conifer. Releases of CO_2 associated with tree care activities account for less than 1% of net CO_2 sequestration.

Air Quality Improvement

Annual air quality benefits

Air quality benefits are defined as the sum of pollutant uptake by trees and avoided power plant emissions due to energy savings minus biogenic volatile organic compounds (BVOCs) released by trees. Average annual air quality benefits over the 40-year period range from $–3 to $1.40 per tree. The negative values for loblolly pines ($–3 per tree) result from this species' emissions of BVOCs (1.1 lbs per year), which may contribute to ozone formation. These high levels exceed the air quality benefits related to other pollutants.

The total average annual air quality benefits are low for the Southern magnolia ($0.31) and the live oak ($0.08)—also emitters of BVOCs. Larger benefits are estimated for the small dogwood, a non-emitter ($1.40 per year). These relatively low air quality benefits also reflect the clean air of most cities in the Coastal Plain region. Contrast these results with the air quality benefits of a large tree in the Midwest region ($7.65; McPherson et al. 2005a), southern California ($28.38; McPherson 2000) or Charlotte, NC ($3.97; McPherson et al. 2005b).

Different species have different air quality benefits

Different species have different air quality strengths. The live oak, for instance, is particularly good at reducing SO_2 and pollutants related to ozone formation. Total O_3 and NO_2 uptake and avoidance for live oak average 1.81 lbs (0.82 kg) per year; SO_2 removal and avoidance averages 2.5 lbs (1.1 kg) per year. The loblolly pine is especially effective at reducing SO_2 and PM_{10}, removing more than a pound (1.41 lb, 0.64 kg) of SO_2 and half a pound (0.41 lb, 0.19 kg) of PM_{10} each year.

Aesthetic and Other Benefits

Aesthetic and other benefits reflected in property values account for the largest portion of total benefits. As trees grow and become more visible, they can increase a property's sales price. Average annual values associated with these aesthetic and other benefits for yard trees are $1, $14, $52, and $24 for the small, medium, and large broadleaf trees and for the conifer, respectively. The values for public trees are $2, $15, $59, and $27, respectively. The values for yard trees are slightly less than for public trees because off-street trees contribute less to a property's curb appeal than more prominent street trees. Because our estimates are based on median home sale prices, the effects of trees on property values and aesthetics will vary depending on local economies.

Aesthetic and other intangible benefits are significant

Chapter 4. Estimating Benefits and Costs for Tree Planting Projects in Your Community

This chapter shows two ways that benefit–cost information presented in this guide can be used. The first hypothetical example demonstrates how to adjust values from the guide for local conditions when the goal is to estimate benefits and costs for a proposed tree planting project. The second example explains how to compare net benefits derived from planting different types of trees. The last section discusses actions communities can take to increase the cost-effectiveness of their tree programs.

Applying Benefit–Cost Data

Cypress Creek Example

The city of Cypress Creek is located in the Coastal Plain region and has a population of 24,000. Most of its street trees were planted decades ago, with live oak (*Quercus virginiana*) and Sabal palmetto

(*Sabal palmetto*) as the dominant species. Currently, the tree canopy cover is sparse because a recent hurricane destroyed many of the trees and they have not been replaced. Many of the remaining street trees are in declining health. The city hired an urban forester two years ago and an active citizens' group, the Green Team, has formed (*Figure 20*).

Initial discussions among the Green Team, local utilities, the urban forester, and other partners led to a proposed urban forestry program. The program intends to plant 1,000 trees in Cypress Creek over a five-year period. Trained volunteers will plant 2-inch (5-cm) diameter trees in the following proportions: 70% large-maturing trees, 15% medium-maturing trees, 5% small-maturing trees and 10% conifers. The total cost for planting will be $120 per tree. One hundred trees will be planted in parks, and the remaining 900 trees will be planted along Main Street and other downtown streets.

The Cypress Creek City Council has agreed to maintain the current funding level for management of existing trees. Also, they will advocate

Figure 20. The Green Team is motivated to re-green their community by planting 1,000 trees in five years.

formation of a municipal tree district to raise funds for the proposed tree-planting project. A municipal tree district is similar in concept to a landscape assessment district, which receives revenues based on formulas that account for the services different customers receive. For example, the proximity of customers to greenspace in a landscape assessment district may determine how much they pay for upkeep. A municipal tree district might receive funding from air quality districts, stormwater management agencies, electric utilities, businesses, and residents in proportion to the value of future benefits these groups will receive from trees in terms of air quality, hydrology, energy, CO_2, and property value. Such a district would require voter approval of a special assessment that charges recipients for tree planting and maintenance costs in proportion to the tangible benefits they receive from the new trees. The Council needs to know the amount of funding required for tree planting and maintenance, as well as how the benefits will be distributed over the 40-year life of the project.

The first step: Determine tree planting numbers and local prices

As a first step, the Cypress Creek city forester and Green Team decided to use the tables in *Appendix B* to quantify total cumulative benefits and costs over 40 years for the proposed planting of 1,000 public trees—700 large, 150 medium, and 50 small broadleaf trees and 100 conifers.

Before setting up a spreadsheet to calculate benefits and costs, the team considered which aspects of Cypress Creek's urban and community forestry project differ from the regional values used in this guide (the methods for calculating the values in *Appendix B* are described in *Appendix C*):

1. The prices of electricity and natural gas in Cypress Creek are $0.11/**kWh** and $0.0150/**kBtu**, not $0.0934/kWh and $0.012/kBtu as assumed in the Guide. It is assumed that the buildings that will be shaded by the new street trees have air conditioning and natural-gas heating.

2. The Green Team projected future annual costs for monitoring tree health and implementing their stewardship program. Administration costs are estimated to average $2,500 annually for the life of the trees or $2.50 per tree each year. This guide assumed an average annual administration cost of $1.78 per tree for large public trees. Thus, an adjustment is necessary.

3. Planting will cost $120 per tree. The Guide assumes planting costs of $150 per tree. The costs will be slightly lower for Cypress Creek because the labor will be provided by trained volunteers.

To calculate the dollar value of total benefits and costs for the 40-year period, the forester created a spreadsheet table (*Table 4*). Each benefit and cost category is listed in the first column. Prices, some adjusted for Cypress Creek and some not, are entered into the second column. The third column contains the **resource units** (RU) per tree per year associated with the benefit or the cost per tree per year, which can be found in *Appendix B*. For aesthetic and other benefits, the dollar values for public trees are placed in the resource unit columns. The fourth column lists the 40-year total values, obtained by multiplying the RU values by tree numbers, prices, and 40 years.

The second step: Adjust for local prices of benefits

To adjust for higher electricity prices, the forester multiplied electricity saved for a large public tree in the RU column (186 kWh) by the Cypress Creek price for electricity ($0.11/kWh). This value ($20.46 per tree per year) was multiplied by the number of trees planted and 40 years ($20.46 × 700 trees × 40 years = $572,880) to obtain cumulative air-conditioning energy savings for the large public trees (*Table 4*). The process was carried out for all benefits and all tree types.

The third step: Adjust for local costs

To adjust cost figures, the city forester changed the planting cost from $150 assumed in the Guide to $120 (*Table 4*). This planting cost was

Table 4. Spreadsheet calculations for the Cypress Creek planting project (1,000 trees). Benefits and costs over 40 years.

| Benefits | Price ($) | 700 large trees | | 150 medium trees | | 50 small trees | | 100 con fer trees | | 1000 total trees | | % of benefits |
		RU/tree/yr	Total $	RU/tree/yr	Total $	RU/tree/yr	Total $	RU/tree/yr	Total $	Total $	$/tree/yr	
Electricity (kWh)	0 110	186	572,880	59	38,940	48	10,560	94	41,360	663,740	16 60	17%
Natural gas (kBtu)	0 015	513	215,460	208	18,720	173	5,190	302	18,120	257,490	6 44	6%
Net CO$_2$ (lb)	0 008	489	102,690	318	14,310	103	1,545	249	7,470	126,015	3 15	3%
Ozone (lb)	1 04	0 88	25,626	0 29	1,810	0 17	354	0 46	1,914	29,702	0 74	
NO$_2$ (lb)	1 04	0 93	27,082	0 33	2,059	0 22	458	0 52	2,163	31,762	0 79	
SO$_2$ (lb)	1 28	2 55	91,392	0 93	7,142	0 63	1,613	1 41	7,219	107,366	2 68	0%
PM$_{10}$ (lb)	0 76	0 63	13,406	0 31	1,414	0 14	213	0 41	1,246	16,279	0 41	
VOCs (lb)	1 48	0 20	8,288	0 07	622	0 05	148	0 11	651	9,709	0 24	
BVOCs (lb)	1 48	-3 95	-163,688	-1 27	-11,278	0 00	0	-4 01	-23,739	-198,705	-4 97	
Hydrology (gal)	0 006	5,699	965,411	1,962	71,221	723	8,748	2,816	68,147	1,113,527	27 84	28%
Aesthetics & other		58 56	1,639,680	15 08	90,480	1 52	3,040	26 77	107,080	1,840,280	46 01	46%
Total benefits			**3,498,226**		**235,439**		**31,868**		**231,632**	**3,997,165**	**104.14**	**100%**

Costs		$/tree/year	Total $	$/tree/year	Total $	$/tree/year	Total $	$/tree/year	Total $	Total $	$/tree/yr	% of costs
Tree & planting		3 00	84,000	3 00	18,000	3 00	6,000	3 00	12,000	120,000	3 00	15%
Pruning		10 27	287,560	8 03	48,180	5 23	10,460	3 17	12,680	358,880	8 97	44%
Remove & dispose		3 55	99,400	2 27	13,620	1 65	3,300	2 80	11,200	127,520	3 19	15%
Infrastructure repair		2 23	62,440	1 42	8,520	1 04	2,080	1 76	7,040	80,080	2 00	10%
Clean-up		1 04	29,120	0 66	3,960	0 49	980	0 82	3,280	37,340	0 93	5%
Admin & other		2 50	70,000	2 50	15,000	2 50	5,000	2 50	10,000	100,000	2 50	12%
Total costs			**632,520**		**107,280**		**27,820**		**56,200**	**823,820**	**20.60**	**100%**
Net benefit		**2,865,706**		**128,159**		**4,048**		**175,432**		**3,173,345**	**79.33**	
Benefit/cost ratio		**5 53**		**2.19**		**1.15**		**4.12**		**4.85**		

RU Resource unit

43

annualized by dividing the cost per tree by 40 years ($120/40 = $3.00 per tree per year). Total planting costs were calculated by multiplying this value by 700 large trees and 40 years ($84,000).

The administration, inspection, and outreach costs are expected to average $2.50 per tree per year, or $100 per tree for the project's life. Consequently, the total administration cost for large trees is $2.50 × 700 large trees × 40 years ($70,000). The same procedure was followed to calculate costs for the medium and small trees and conifers.

The fourth step: Calculate net benefits and benefit–cost ratios for public trees

Subtracting total costs from total benefits yields net benefits:

- Large broadleaf trees: $2,865,706 over 40 years or $102.35 per tree per year

- Medium broadleaf trees: $128,159 or $21.36 per tree per year

- Small broadleaf trees: $4,048 or $2.02 per tree per year

- Conifers: $175,432 or $43.86 per tree per year

Annual benefits over 40 years total nearly $4 million ($104 per tree per year), and annual costs total a less than $1 million ($21 per tree per year). The total net annual benefits for all 1,000 trees over the 40-year period are $3.2 million, or $84 per tree. To calculate the average annual net benefit per tree, the forester divided the total net benefit by the number of trees planted (1,000) and 40 years ($3,173,345 / 1,000 trees / 40 years = $79.33). Dividing total benefits by total costs yielded benefit–cost ratios (BCRs) that ranged from 1.15 for small trees, to 2.19, 5.53 and 4.12 for medium and large broadleaf trees and conifers. The BCR for the entire planting is 4.85, indicating that $4.85 will be returned for every $1 invested.

This analysis assumes 35% of the planted trees die and does not account for the time value of money from a capital investment perspective. Use the municipal discount rate to compare this investment in tree planting and management with alternative municipal investments.

The final step: Determine how benefits are distributed and link these to sources of revenue

The city forester and Green Team now know that the project will cost about $825,000, and the average annual cost will be $20,625 ($825,000 / 40 years); however, a higher proportion of funds will be needed initially for planting and irrigation. The fifth and last step is to identify the distribution of functional benefits that the trees will provide. The last column in *Table 4* shows the distribution of benefits as a percentage of the total:

- Energy savings = 23% (cooling = 17%, heating = 6%)

- Carbon dioxide reduction = 3%

- Stormwater runoff reduction = 28%

- Aesthetics/property value increase = 46%

With this information the planning team can determine how to distribute the costs for tree planting and maintenance based on who benefits from the services the trees will provide. For example, assuming the goal is to generate enough annual revenue to cover the total costs of managing the trees ($825,000), fees could be distributed in the following manner:

Distributing costs of tree management to multiple parties

- $181,500 from electric and natural gas utilities for energy savings (23%)

- $24,750 from local industry for atmospheric carbon dioxide reductions (3%)

- $222,750 from the stormwater management district for water quality improvement associated with reduced runoff (28%)

- $363,000 from property owners for increased property values (46%)

Whether funds are sought from partners, the general fund, or other sources, this information can assist managers in developing policy, setting priorities, and making decisions. The Center for Urban Forest Research has developed a computer program called STRATUM that simplifies these calculations for analysis of existing street tree populations (Maco and McPherson 2003; www.itreetools.org).

City of Tillandsia Example

As a municipal cost-cutting measure, the city of Tillandsia plans to stop planting street trees in areas of new development. Instead, developers will be required to plant front yard trees, thereby reducing costs to the city. The community forester and concerned citizens believe that, although this policy will result in lower planting costs, developers may plant smaller trees than the city would have. Currently, Tillandsia's policy is to plant as large a tree as possible based on each site's available growing space (*Figure 21*). Planting smaller trees could result in benefits "forgone" that will exceed cost savings. To evaluate this possible outcome the community forester and concerned citizens decided to compare costs and benefits of planting large, medium, and small trees for a hypothetical street-tree planting project in Tillandsia.

As a first step, the city forester and concerned citizens decided to quantify the total cumulative benefits and costs over 40 years for a typical street tree planting of 1,500 trees in Tillandsia. For comparison purposes, the planting includes 500 large trees, 500 medium trees, and 500 small trees. Data in *Appendix B* are used for the calculations;

The first step: Determine tree numbers and local prices

however, three aspects of Tillandsia's urban and community forestry program are different than assumed in this tree guide:

1. The price of electricity is $0.075/kWh, not $0.0934/kWh.

2. The trees will be irrigated for the first five years at a cost of approximately $0.50 per tree annually.

3. Planting costs are $175 per tree for city trees instead of $150 per tree.

The second step: Calculate benefits and costs over 40 years

To calculate the dollar value of total benefits and costs for the 40-year period, the last column in *Appendix B* (40-year average) is multiplied by 40 years. Since this value is for one tree it must be multiplied by the total number of trees planted in the respective large, medium, or small tree size classes. To adjust for lower electricity prices we multiply electricity saved for each tree type in the resource unit column by the number of trees and 40 years (large tree: 186 kWh × 500 trees × 40 years = 3,720,000 kWh). This value is multiplied by the price of electricity in Tillandsia ($0.075/kWh × 3,720,000 kWh = $279,000) to obtain cumulative air-conditioning energy savings for the project (*Table 5*).

Figure 21. Tillandsia's policy to plant as large a tree as the site will handle has provided ample benefits in the past. Here, a large-stature tree has been planted.

All the benefits are summed for each size tree for a 40-year period. The 500 large trees provide $2.4 million in total benefits. The medium and small trees provide approximately $720,000 and $285,000, respectively.

The third step: Adjust for local costs

To adjust cost figures, we add a value for irrigation by multiplying the annual cost by the number of trees by the number of years that irrigation will be applied ($0.50 × 500 trees × 5 years = $1,250). We multiply 500 large trees by the unit planting cost ($175) to obtain the adjusted cost for planting (500 × $175 = $87,500). The average annual 40-year costs taken from *Appendix B* for other items are multiplied by 40 years and the appropriate number of trees to compute total costs. These 40-year cost values are entered into *Table 5*.

The fourth step: Calculate the net benefits

Subtracting total costs from total benefits yields net benefits for the large ($1,902,450), medium ($359,450), and small ($11,250) trees. The total net benefits for the 40-year period are $2.27 million (total benefits – total costs), or $1,515 per tree ($2.27 million/1,500 trees) on average (*Table 5*).

Table 5. Spreadsheet calculations for the Tillandsia planting project (1,500 trees). Benefits and costs over 40 years.

Benefits	500 large trees		500 medium trees		500 small trees		1,500 tree total	
	RUs	Total $	RUs	Total $	RUs	Total $	RUs	Total $
Electricity (kWh)	3,720,000	279,000	1,180,000	88,600	960,000	72,000	5,860,000	439,600
Natural gas (kBtu)	10,260,000	154,000	4,160,000	62,400	3,460,000	52,000	17,880,000	268,400
Net CO_2 (lb)	9,780,000	73,400	2,980,000	22,400	2,060,000	15,400	14,820,000	111,200
Ozone (lb)	17,510	18,200	5,820	6,000	3,480	3,600	26,810	27,800
NO_2 (lb)	18,570	19,400	6,650	7,000	4,500	4,600	29,720	31,000
SO_2 (lb)	51,010	65,400	18,680	24,000	12,620	16,200	82,310	105,600
PM10 (lb)	12,620	9,600	6,140	4,600	2,720	2,000	21,480	16,200
VOCs (lb)	3,910	5,800	1,440	2,200	1,000	1,400	6,350	9,400
BVOCs (lb)	-78,900	-117,000	-25,330	-37,600	0	0	-104,230	-154,600
Hydrology (gal)	113,980,000	689,600	39,240,000	237,400	14,460,000	87,400	167,680,000	1,014,400
Aesthetics and other benefits		1,171,200		301,600		30,400		1,503,200
Total benefits		**2,368,600**		**718,600**		**285,000**		**3,372,200**
Costs		Total $		Total $		Total $		Total $
Tree & planting		87,500		87,500		87,500		262,500
Pruning		205,400		160,600		104,600		470,600
Remove & dispose		71,000		45,400		33,000		149,400
Infrastructure		44,600		28,400		20,800		93,800
Irrigation		1,250		1,250		1,250		3,750
Clean-up		20,800		13,200		9,800		43,800
Admin & other		35,600		22,800		16,800		75,200
Total costs		**466,150**		**359,150**		**273,750**		**1,099,050**
Net benefits		**1,902,450**		**359,450**		**11,250**		**2,273,150**
Benefit /Cost ratio		**5.08**		**2.00**		**1.04**		**3.07**

RU Resource unit

The net benefits per public tree planted are as follows:

- $3,804 for a large tree

- $719 for a medium tree

- $23 for a small tree

The fifth step: Calculate cost savings and benefits forgone

By not investing in street tree planting, the city would save $262,500 in initial planting costs. If the developer planted 1,500 small trees, benefits would total $855,000 (3 x $285,000 for 500 small trees). If 1,500 large trees were planted, benefits would total $7.1 million. Planting all small trees causes the city to forgo benefits valued at $6.25 million. This amount far exceeds the savings of $262,500 obtained by requiring developers to plant new street trees, and suggests that the City should review developers' planting plans to maintain the policy of planting large trees where feasible.

Based on this analysis, the City of Tillandsia decided to retain the policy of promoting planting of large trees where space permits. They now require tree shade plans that show how developers will achieve 50% shade over streets, sidewalks, and parking lots within 15 years of development.

This analysis assumed 35% of the planted trees died. It did not account for the time value of money from a capital investment perspective, but this could be done using the municipal discount rate.

Increasing Program Cost-Effectiveness

What if costs are too high?

What if the program you have designed is promising in terms of stormwater-runoff reduction, energy savings, volunteer participation, and additional benefits, but the costs are too high? This section describes some steps to consider that may increase benefits and reduce costs, thereby increasing cost-effectiveness.

Increasing Benefits

Work to increase survival rates

Improved stewardship to increase the health and survival of recently planted trees is one strategy for increasing cost-effectiveness. An evaluation of the Sacramento Shade program found that tree survival rates had a substantial impact on projected benefits (Hildebrandt et al. 1996). Higher survival rates increase energy savings and reduce tree removal and planting costs.

Target tree plantings with highest return

Conifers and broadleaf evergreens intercept rainfall and particulate matter year-round as well as reduce wind speeds and provide shade, which lowers summer-cooling and winter-heating costs. Locating these types of trees in yards, parks, school grounds, and other open-space areas can increase benefits.

You can further increase energy benefits by planting a higher percentage of trees in locations that produce the greatest energy savings, such as opposite west-facing walls and close to buildings with air conditioning. Keep in mind that evergreen trees, as demonstrated in this study by the live oak, Southern magnolia and the loblolly pine, should not be planted on the southern side of buildings because their branches and leaves block the warm rays of the winter sun. By customizing tree locations to increase numbers in high-yield sites, energy savings can be boosted.

Customize planting locations

Reducing Program Costs

Cost effectiveness is influenced by program costs as well as benefits:

Cost-effectiveness = Total net benefit / total program cost

Cutting costs is one strategy to increase cost effectiveness. A substantial percentage of total program costs occur during the first five years and are associated with tree planting and establishment (McPherson 1993). Some strategies to reduce these costs include:

Reduce up-front and establishment costs

- Plant bare-root or smaller tree stock.

- Use trained volunteers for planting and pruning of young trees (*Figure 22*).

- Provide follow-up care to increase tree survival and reduce replacement costs.

- Select and locate trees to avoid conflicts with infrastructure.

Where growing conditions are likely to be favorable, such as yard or garden settings, it may be cost-effective to use smaller, less expensive stock or bare-root trees. In highly urbanized settings and sites subject to vandalism, however, large stock may survive the initial establishment period better than small stock.

Use less expensive stock where appropriate

Investing in the resources needed to promote tree establishment during the first five years after planting is usually worthwhile, because once trees are established they have a high probability of continued survival. If your program has targeted trees on private property, then encourage residents to attend tree-care workshops. Develop standards of "establishment success" for different types of tree species. Perform periodic inspections to alert residents to tree health problems, and reward those whose trees meet your program's establishment standards. Replace dead trees as soon as possible, and identify ways to improve survivability.

Early investment pays off

Although organizing and training volunteers requires labor and resources, it is usually less costly than contracting the work, and it can

Train volunteers to monitor tree health and to do early pruning

help build more support for your program. A cadre of trained volunteers can easily maintain trees until they reach a height of about 20 ft (6 m) and limbs are too high to prune from the ground with pole pruners. By the time trees reach this size they are well established. Pruning during this establishment period should result in trees that will require less care in the long term. Training young trees can provide a strong branching structure that requires less frequent thinning and shaping (Costello 2000). Ideally, young trees should be inspected and pruned every other year for the first five years after planting.

Prune early

As trees grow larger, pruning costs may increase on a per-tree basis. The frequency of pruning will influence these costs, since it takes longer to prune a tree that has not been pruned in 10 years than one that was pruned a few years ago. Although pruning frequency varies by species and location, a return frequency of about five to eight years is usually sufficient for older trees (Miller 1997).

Figure 22. Trained volunteers can plant and maintain young trees, allowing the community to accomplish more at less cost and providing satisfaction for participants. (Photo courtesy of Tree Trust)

Carefully select and locate trees to avoid conflicts with overhead power lines, sidewalks, and underground utilities. Time spent planning the planting will result in long-term savings. Also consider soil type and irrigation, microclimate, and the type of activities occurring around the tree that will influence its growth and management.

Match tree to site

When evaluating the bottom line—trees pay us back—do not forget to consider benefits other than the stormwater–runoff reductions, energy savings, atmospheric CO_2 reductions, and other tangible benefits. The magnitude of benefits related to employment opportunities, job training, community building, reduced violence, and enhanced human health and well-being can be substantial (*Figure 23*). Moreover, these benefits extend beyond the site where trees are planted, furthering collaborative efforts to build better communities.

It all adds up—trees pay us back

For more information on urban and community forestry program design and implementation, see the list of additional resources in *Appendix A*.

Figure 23. Trees pay us back in tangible and intangible ways.

Chapter 5. General Guidelines for Selecting and Placing Trees

In this chapter, general guidelines for selecting and locating trees are presented. Residential trees and trees in public places are considered.

Guidelines for Energy Savings

Maximizing Energy Savings from Shading

The right tree in the right place can save energy and reduce tree care costs. In midsummer, the sun shines on the east side of a building in the morning, passes over the roof near midday, and then shines on the west side in the afternoon (see *Figure 4*). Electricity use is highest during the afternoon when temperatures are warmest and incoming sunshine is greatest. Therefore, the west side of a home is the most important side to shade (Sand 1994).

Where should shade trees be planted?

Depending on building orientation and window placement, sun shining through windows can heat a home quickly during the morning hours. The east side is the second most important side to shade when considering the net impact of tree shade on energy savings (*Figure 24*). Deciduous trees on the east side provide summer shade and more winter solar heat gain than evergreens.

Figure 24. Locate trees to shade west and east windows (from Sand 1993).

Trees located to shade south walls can block winter sunshine and increase heating costs because during winter the sun is lower in the sky and shines on the south side of homes (*Figure 25*). The warmth the sun provides is an asset, so do not plant evergreen trees that will block southern exposures and solar collectors. Use solar-friendly trees to the south because the bare branches of these deciduous trees allow most sunlight to strike the building (some solar-unfriendly deciduous

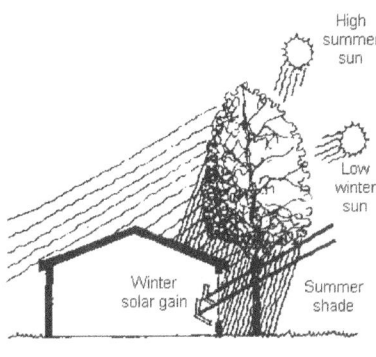

Figure 25. Select solar-friendly trees for southern exposures and locate them close enough to provide winter solar access and summer shade (from Sand 1991).

Figure 26. Trees south of a home before and after pruning. Lower branches are pruned up to increase heat gain from winter sun (from Sand 1993).

trees can reduce sunlight striking the south side of buildings by 50% even without leaves) (Ames 1987). Examples of solar-friendly trees include most species and cultivars of maples (*Acer* spp.), crapemyrtle (*Lagerstroemia indica*), honey locust (*Gleditsia triacanthos*), sweetgum (*Liquidamber styraciflua*), and zelkova (*Zelkova serrata*). Some solar-unfriendly trees include most oaks (*Quercus* spp.), sycamore (*Platanus* spp.), most elms (*Ulmus* spp.), and river birch (*Betula nigra*) (McPherson et al. 1994).

To maximize summer shade and minimize winter shade, locate shade trees about 10–20 ft (3–6 m) south of the home. As trees grow taller, prune lower branches to allow more sun to reach the building if this will not weaken the tree's structure (*Figure 26*).

Although the closer a tree is to a home the more shade it provides, roots of trees that are too close can damage the foundation. Branches that impinge on the building can make it difficult to maintain exterior walls and windows. Keep trees 10 ft (3 m) or further from the home depending on mature crown spread, to avoid these conflicts. Trees within 30–50 ft (9–15 m) of the home most effectively shade windows and walls.

Patios, driveways and air conditioners need shade

Paved patios and driveways can become **heat sinks** that warm the home during the day. Shade trees can make them cooler and more comfortable spaces. If a home is equipped with an air conditioner, shading can reduce its energy use, but do not plant vegetation so close that it will obstruct the flow of air around the unit.

Avoid power, sewer, and water lines

Plant only small-growing trees under overhead power lines and avoid planting directly above underground water and sewer lines if possible. Contact your local utility company before planting to determine where underground lines are located and which tree species should not be planted below power lines.

Planting Windbreaks for Heating Savings

A tree's size and crown density can make it ideal for blocking wind, thereby reducing the impacts of winter weather and storms. However, unimpeded air flow is desired for natural cooling during summer months. If prevailing winter and summer winds are from different directions, locate rows of trees perpendicular to the prevailing winter winds. If prevailing winds are from the same direction, do not obstruct cooling summer breezes with windbreak plantings.

If your site can benefit from a windbreak, design the row to be longer than the building being sheltered because wind speed increases at the edge of the windbreak. Ideally, the windbreak should be planted upwind about 25–50 ft (7–15 m) from the building and should consist of evergreens that will grow to twice the height of the building they shelter (Heisler 1986; Sand 1991). Trees should be spaced close enough to form a dense screen, but not so close that they will block sunlight to each other, causing lower branches to self-prune. Most conifers can be spaced about 6 ft (2 m) on center. If there is room for two or more rows, then space rows 10–12 ft (3–4 m) apart.

Trees for Hurricane-Prone Areas

In addition to damage caused to urban infrastructure, hurricanes can also have a significant impact on a city's green infrastructure. Trees may be uprooted, snapped, or may lose large branches. But hurricanes don't affect all trees or all tree species equally. A study in Florida after two hurricanes in the summer of 1995 showed that some species stood a better chance of surviving (Duryea 1997). The most wind resistant trees were dogwood, live oak, sabal palm (*Sabal palmetto*), sand live oak (*Quercus geminata*) and Southern magnolia. The least wind resistant were sand pine and Carolina laurelcherry (*Prunus caroliniana*). Other studies have shown pond and bald cypress to be extremely wind resistant (Ogden 1992).

Some species are more wind-resistant than others

Look for native trees—they have stood the test of time. Preferred species have wide spreading branches, strong, deep root systems, low centers of gravity, and small leaves. Prune trees appropriately to remove weak branches and improve structure. (See http://hort.ifas.ufl.edu/woody/pruning/index.htm for extensive information on pruning.)

Native trees have stood the test of countless hurricanes

Selecting Trees to Maximize Benefits

The ideal shade tree has a fairly dense, round crown with limbs broad enough to partially shade the roof. Given the same placement, a large tree will provide more shade than a small tree. Deciduous trees allow sun to shine through leafless branches in winter. Plant small trees where nearby buildings or power lines limit aboveground space. Columnar trees are appropriate in narrow side yards. Because the best location for shade trees is relatively close to the west and east sides of buildings, the most suitable trees will be strong and capable of resisting storm damage, disease, and pests (Sand 1994). Examples of trees not to select for placement near buildings include cottonwoods (*Populus* spp.) and silver maple (*Acer saccharinum*) because of their invasive roots, weak wood, and large size, and ginkgos (*Ginkgo biloba*) because of their sparse shade and slow growth.

Picking the right tree

When selecting trees, match the tree's water requirements with those of surrounding plants. For instance, select low water-use species for planting in areas that receive little irrigation. Also, match the tree's maintenance requirements with the amount of care and the type of use different areas in the landscape receive. For instance, tree species that drop fruit that can be a slip-and-fall problem should not be planted near paved areas that are frequently used by pedestrians. Check with your local landscape professional before selecting trees to make sure that they are well suited to the site's soil and climatic conditions.

Maximizing energy savings from trees

Use the following practices to plant and manage trees strategically to maximize energy conservation benefits:

- Increase community-wide tree canopy, and target shade to streets, parking lots, and other paved surfaces, as well as air-conditioned buildings.

- Shade west- and east-facing windows and walls.

- Avoid planting trees to the south of buildings.

- Select solar-friendly trees opposite east- and south-facing walls.

- Shade air conditioners, but don't obstruct air flow.

- Avoid planting trees too close to utilities and buildings.

- Create multi-row, evergreen windbreaks where space permits, that are longer than the building.

Guidelines for Reducing Carbon Dioxide

Select trees well suited to the site

Because trees in common areas and other public places may not shelter buildings from sun and wind and reduce energy use, CO_2 reductions are primarily due to sequestration. Fast-growing trees sequester more CO_2 initially than slow-growing trees, but this advantage can be lost if the fast-growing trees die at younger ages. Large trees have the capacity to store more CO_2 than smaller trees (*Figure 27*). To maxi-

Figure 27. Compared with small trees, large trees can store more carbon, filter more air pollutants, intercept more rainfall, and provide greater energy savings.

mize CO_2 sequestration, select tree species that are well suited to the site where they will be planted. Consult with your local arborist to select the right tree for your site. Trees that are not well adapted will grow slowly, show symptoms of stress, or die at an early age. Unhealthy trees do little to reduce atmospheric CO_2 and can be unsightly liabilities in the landscape.

Design and management guidelines that can increase CO_2 reductions include the following:

- Maximize use of woody plants, especially trees, as they store more CO_2 than do herbaceous plants and grasses.

- Plant more trees where feasible and immediately replace dead trees to compensate for CO_2 lost through removal.

- Create diverse habitats, with trees of different ages and species, to promote a continuous canopy cover over time.

- Group species with similar landscape maintenance requirements together and consider how irrigation, pruning, fertilization, weed, pest, and disease control can be minimized.

- Reduce CO_2 associated with landscape management by using push mowers (not gas or electric), hand saws (not chain saws), pruners (not gas/electric shears), rakes (not leaf blowers), and employ landscape professionals who don't have to travel far to your site.

- Reduce maintenance by reducing turfgrass and planting drought-tolerant or environmentally friendly landscapes.

Maximizing CO_2 sequestration

57

- Consider the project's life span when selecting species. Fast-growing species will sequester more CO_2 initially than slow-growing species, but may not live as long.

- Provide ample space belowground for tree roots to grow so that they can maximize CO_2 sequestration and tree longevity.

- When trees die or are removed, salvage as much wood as possible for use as furniture and other long-lasting products to delay decomposition.

- Plant trees, shrubs, and vines in strategic locations to maximize summer shade and reduce winter shade, thereby reducing atmospheric CO_2 emissions associated with power production.

Guidelines for Reducing Stormwater Runoff

Trees are mini-reservoirs, controlling runoff at the source because their leaves and branch surfaces intercept and store rainfall, thereby reducing runoff volumes and erosion of watercourses, as well as delaying the onset of peak flows. Rainfall interception by large trees is a relatively inexpensive first line of defense in the battle to control nonpoint-source pollution.

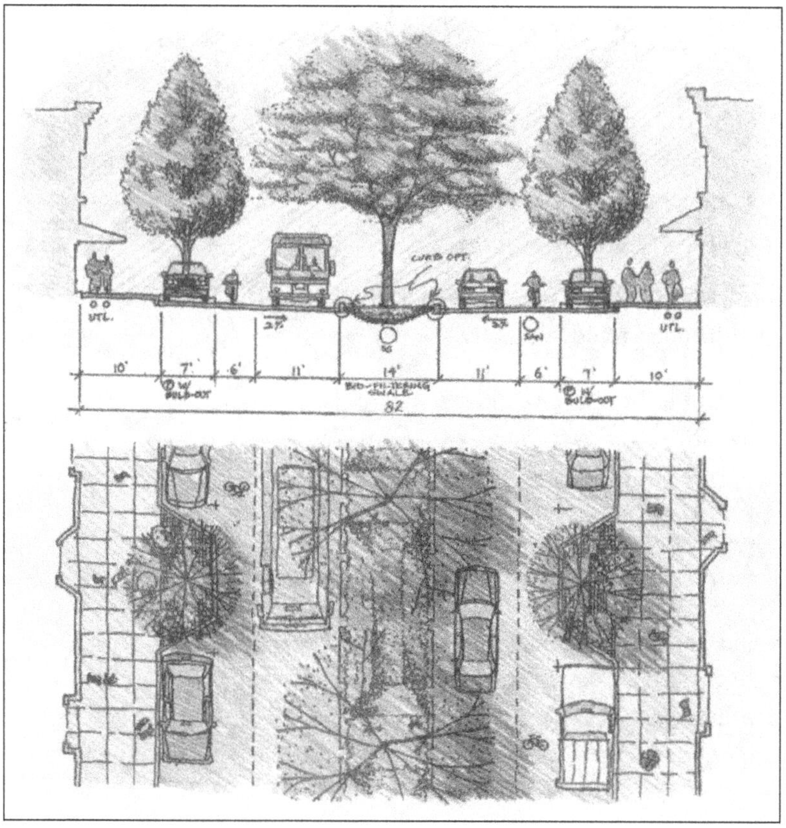

When selecting trees to maximize rainfall interception benefits, consider the following:

- Select tree species with physiological features that maximize interception, such as large leaf surface area and rough surfaces that store water (Metro 2002).

- Increase interception by planting large trees where possible (*Figure 28*).

- Plant trees that are in leaf when precipitation levels are highest.

- Select conifers because they have high interception rates, but avoid shading south-facing windows to maximize solar heat gain in winter.

Figure 28. Trees can create a continuous canopy for maximum rainfall interception, even in commercial areas. In this example, a swale in the median filters runoff and provides ample space for large trees. Parking space-sized planters contain the soil volume required to grow healthy, large trees (from Metro 2002).

- Plant low-water-use tree species where appropriate and native species that, once established, require little supplemental irrigation.

- In bioretention areas, such as roadside swales, select species that tolerate inundation, are long-lived, wide-spreading, and fast-growing (Metro 2002).

- Do not pave over streetside planting strips for easier weed control; this can reduce tree health and increase runoff.

- Bioswales in parking lots and other paved areas store and filter stormwater while providing good conditions for trees.

Guidelines for Improving Air Quality Benefits

Trees, sometimes called the "lungs of our cities," are important because of their ability to remove contaminants from the air. The amount of gaseous pollutants and particulates removed by trees depends on their size and architecture, as well as local meteorology and pollutant concentrations.

Along streets, in parking lots, and in commercial areas, locate trees to maximize shade on paving and parked vehicles. Shade trees reduce heat that is stored or reflected by paved surfaces. By cooling streets and parking areas, trees reduce emissions of evaporative hydrocarbons from parked cars and thereby reduce smog formation (Scott et al. 1999). Large trees can shade a greater area than smaller trees, but should be used only where space permits. Remember that a tree needs space for both branches and roots.

Tree planting and management guidelines to improve air quality include the following (Smith and Dochinger 1976; Nowak 2000):

Maximizing air pollutant uptake and avoidance with trees

- Select species that tolerate pollutants that are present in harmful concentrations. For example, in areas with high O_3 concentration avoid sensitive species such as white and green ash (*Fraxinus americana* and *F. pennsylvanica*), tulip tree (*Liriodendron tulipifera*), and Austrian pine (*Pinus nigra*) (Noble et al. 1988).

- Conifers have high surface-to-volume ratios and retain their foliage year-round, which may make them more effective than deciduous species.

- Species with long leaf stems (e.g., ash, maple) and hairy plant parts (e.g., oak, birch, sumac) are especially efficient interceptors.

- Effective uptake depends on proximity to the pollutant source and the amount of biomass. Where space permits, plant multi-layered stands near the source of pollutants.

- Consider the local meteorology and topography to promote air flow that can "flush" pollutants at night and avoid trapping them in the urban canopy layer during the day.

- In areas with unhealthy ozone concentrations, maximize use of plants that emit low levels of BVOCs to reduce ozone formation.

- Sustain large, healthy trees; they produce the most benefits.

- To reduce emissions of VOCs and other pollutants, plant trees to shade parked cars and conserve energy.

Guidelines for Avoiding Conflicts with Infrastructure

Trees can become liabilities when they conflict with power lines, underground utilities, and other infrastructure elements. Guidelines to reduce conflicts with infrastructure include the following:

- Before planting, contact your local before-digging company, such as PUPS, the Utilities Protection Center, or One Call, to locate underground water, sewer, gas, and telecommunications lines.

- Avoid locating trees where they will block streetlights or views of traffic and commercial signs.

- Check with local transportation officials for sight visibility requirements. Keep trees at least 30 ft (10 m) away from street intersections to ensure visibility.

Match each tree to its site

- Avoid planting shallow-rooting species near sidewalks, curbs, and paving where tree roots can heave pavement if planted too close. Generally, avoid planting within 3 ft (1 m) of pavement, and remember that trunk flare at the base of large trees can displace soil and paving for a considerable distance. Consider strategies to reduce damage by tree roots such as meandering sidewalks around trees (Costello and Jones 2003).

- Select only small trees (<25 ft tall [8 m]) for location under overhead power lines, and do not plant directly above underground water and sewer lines (*Figure 29*). Avoid locating trees where they will block illumination from streetlights or views of street signs in parking lots, commercial areas, and along streets.

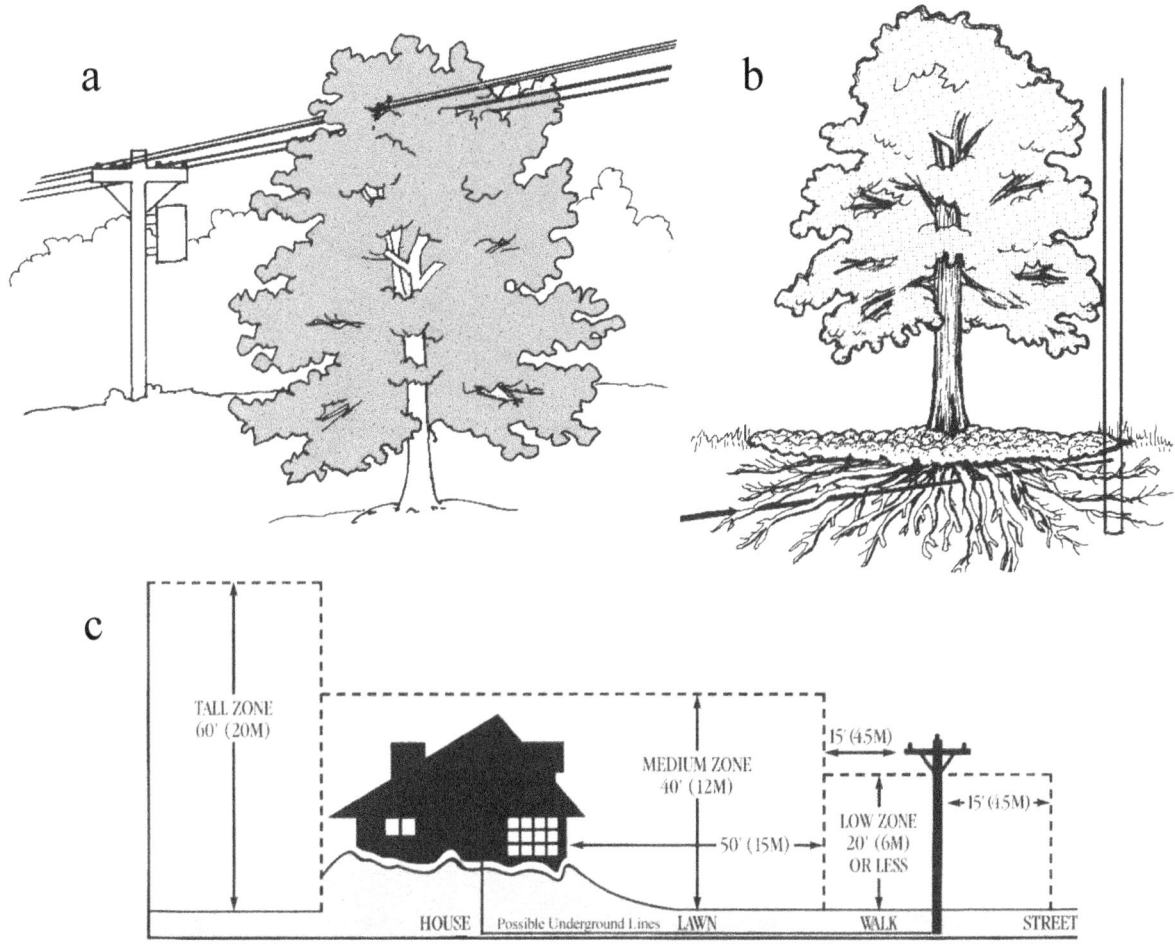

a

b

c

TALL ZONE
60' (20M)

MEDIUM ZONE
40' (12M)

15' (4.5M)

LOW ZONE
20' (6M)
OR LESS

15' (4.5M)

50' (15M)

HOUSE   Possible Underground Lines   LAWN   WALK   STREET

Figure 29. (a,b) Know where power lines and other utility lines are before planting. (c) Under power lines use only small-growing trees ("low zone") and avoid planting directly above underground utilities. Larger trees may be planted where space permits ("medium" and "tall zones") (from ISA 1992).

For trees to deliver benefits over the long term they require enough soil volume to grow and remain healthy. Matching tree species to the site's soil volume can reduce sidewalk and curb damage as well. *Figure 30* shows recommended soil volumes for different sized trees.

Maintenance requirements and public safety concerns influence the type of trees selected for public places. The ideal public tree is not susceptible to wind damage and branch drop, does not require frequent pruning, produces negligible litter, is deep-rooted, has few serious pest and disease problems, and tolerates a wide range of soil conditions, irrigation regimes, and air pollutants. Because relatively few trees have all these traits, it is important to match the tree species to the planting site by determining what issues are most important on a case-by-case basis. For example, parking-lot trees should be tolerant of hot, dry conditions, have strong branch attachments, and be resistant to attacks by pests that leave vehicles covered with sticky

SOIL VOLUME FOR TREES

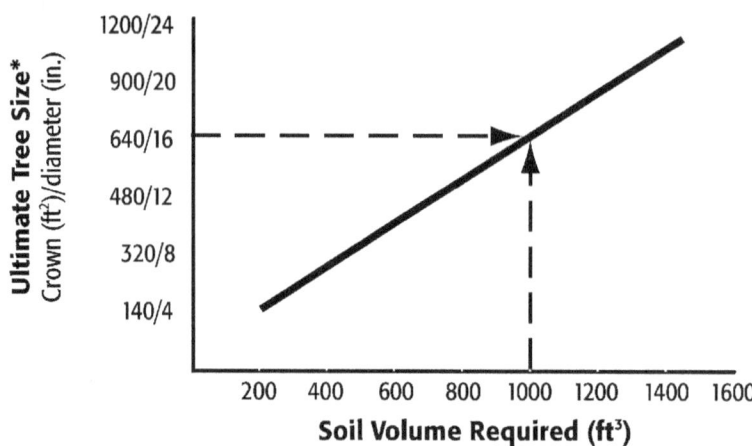

Figure 30. Developed from several sources by Urban (1992), this graph shows the relationship between tree size and required soil volume. For example, a tree with a 16-inch diameter at breast height (41 cm) with 640 ft² of crown projection area (59.5 m² under the drip-line) requires 1,000 ft³ (28 m³) of soil (from Costello and Jones 2003).

exudates. Check with your local landscape professional for horticultural information on tree traits.

Guidelines for Maximizing Long-Term Benefits

Selecting a tree from the nursery that has a high probability of becoming a healthy, trouble-free **mature tree** is critical to a successful outcome. Therefore, select the very best stock at your nursery, and when necessary, reject nursery stock that does not meet industry standards.

The root ball is critical to survival

The health of the tree's root ball is critical to its ultimate survival. If the tree is in a container, check for matted roots by sliding off the container. Roots should penetrate to the edge of the root ball, but not densely circle the inside of the container or grow through drain holes. As well, at least two large structural roots should emerge from the trunk within 1–3 inches (2–7 cm) of the soil surface. If there are no roots in the upper portion of the root ball, it is undersized and the tree should not be planted.

A good tree is well anchored

Another way to evaluate the quality of the tree before planting is to gently move the trunk back and forth. A good tree trunk bends and does not move in the soil, while a poor trunk bends a little and pivots at or below the soil line—a tell-tale sign of a poorly anchored tree.

Dig the planting hole 1 inch (2.5 cm) shallower than the depth of the root ball to allow for some settling after watering. Make the hole two to three times as wide as the root ball and loosen the sides of the hole to make it easier for roots to penetrate. Place the tree so that the root flare is at the top of the soil. If the structural roots have grown properly as described above, the top of the root ball will be slightly higher (1–2 inches) than the surrounding soil to allow for settling. Backfill with the native soil unless it is very rocky or sandy, in which case

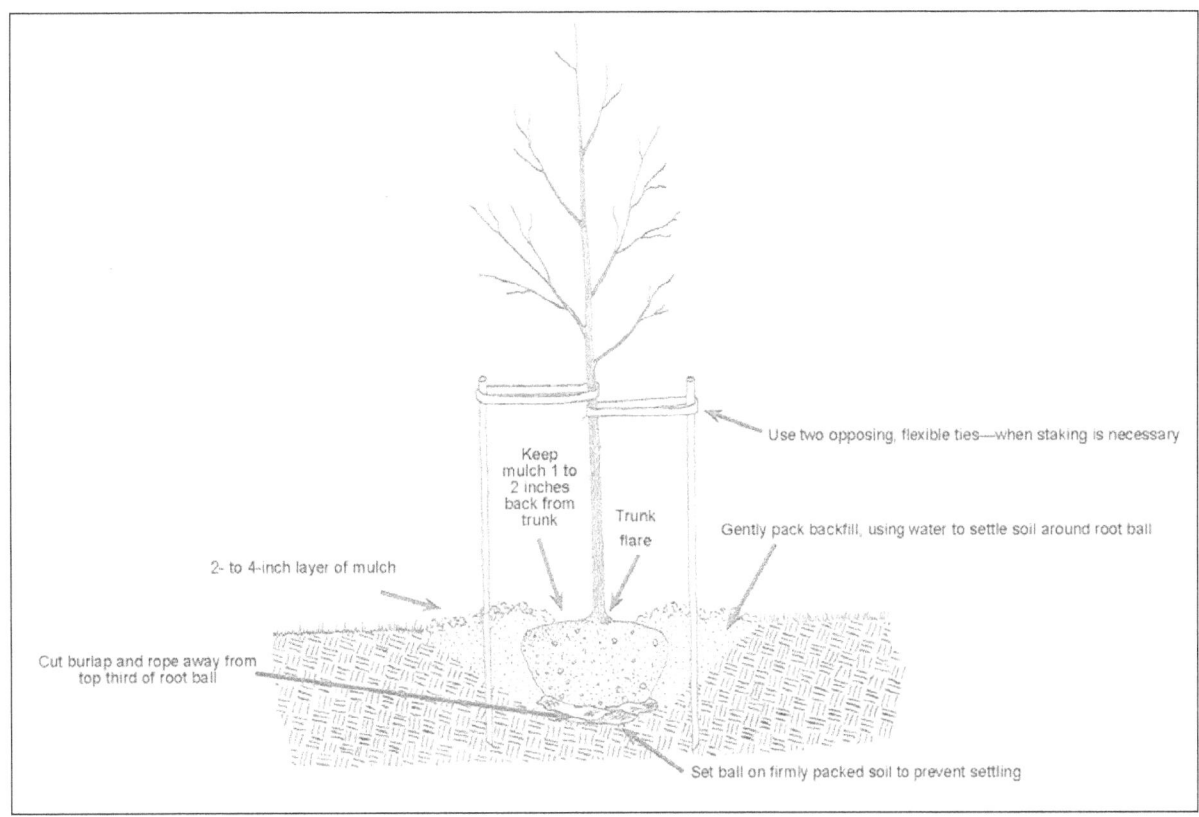

Figure 31. Prepare a broad planting area, plant the tree with the root flare at ground level, and provide a berm/water ring to retain water (drawing courtesy of ISA).

you may want to add composted organic matter such as peat moss or shredded bark (*Figure 31*).

Expect additional planting challenges in urban areas

Planting trees in urban plazas, commercial areas, and parking lots poses special challenges due to limited soil volume and poor soil structure. Engineered or structural soils can be placed under the hardscape to increase rooting space while meeting engineering requirements. For more information on structural soils see *Reducing Infrastructure Damage by Tree Roots: A Compendium of Strategies* (Costello and Jones 2003).

Use the extra soil left after planting to build a berm outside the root ball that is 6 in (15 cm) high and 3 ft (1 m) in diameter. Soak the tree, and gently rock it to settle it in. Cover the basin with a 2- to 4-in (10-cm) thick layer of mulch, but avoid placing mulch against the tree trunk. Water the new tree three times a week and increase the amount of water as the tree grows larger. Generally, a tree requires about 1 inch (2.5 cm) of water per week. A rain gauge or soil moisture sensor (tensiometer) can help determine tree watering needs.

After you've planted your tree, remember the following:

Don't forget about the tree

- Inspect your tree several times a year, and contact a local landscape professional if problems develop.

- If your tree needed staking to keep it upright, remove the stake and ties after one year or as soon as the tree can hold itself up. The staking should allow some tree movement, as this movement sends hormones to the roots causing them to grow and create greater tree stability. It also promotes trunk taper and growth.

- Reapply mulch and irrigate the tree as needed.

- Leave lower side branches on young trees for the first year and prune back to 4–6 inches (10–15 cm) to accelerate tree diameter development. Remove these lateral branches after the first full year. Prune the young tree to maintain a central main trunk and equally spaced branches. For more information, see Costello (2000) and Gilman (2002). As the tree matures, have it pruned on a regular basis by a certified arborist or other experienced professional.

- By keeping your tree healthy, you maximize its ability to produce shade, intercept rainfall, reduce atmospheric CO_2, and provide other benefits.

For more information on tree selection, planting, establishment, and care see the resources listed in Appendix A.

Appendix A: Additional Resources

Additional information regarding urban and community forestry program design and implementation can be obtained from the following sources:

Bratkovich, S.M. 2001. *Utilizing municipal trees: ideas from across the country.* NA-TP-06-01. Newtown Square, PA: U.S. Department of Agriculture, Forest Service, Northeastern Area State and Private Forestry.

Hartel, D.R., coord. author. 2005. *The Urban Forestry Manual. A Manual for Urban Forestry in the South.* Athens, GA: U.S. Department of Agriculture, Forest Service, Southern Center for Urban Forestry Research & Information

Miller, R.W. 1997. *Urban forestry: planning and managing urban greenspaces.* 2nd Edition. Upper Saddle River, NJ: Prentice-Hall.

Morgan, N.R. 1993. *A technical guide to urban and community forestry.* Portland, OR: World Forestry Center.

Pokorny, J.D., coord. author. 2003. *Urban tree risk management: a community guide to program design and implementation.* NA-TP-03-03. Newtown Square, PA: U.S. Department of Agriculture, Forest Service, Northeastern Area State and Private Forestry.

For additional information on tree selection, planting, establishment, and care see the following resources:

Alliance for Community Trees: http://actrees.org

Arboriculture (Harris et al. 1999)

Bedker, P.J.; O'Brien, J.G.; Mielke, M.E. 1995. *How to prune trees.* NA-FR-01-95. Newtown Square, PA: U.S. Department of Agriculture, Forest Service, Northeastern Area State and Private Forestry.

The Bugwood Network. http://www.bugwood.org. The website of this collaborative working group headed by the University of Georgia offers links and vast resources for information on Southern tree pests and diseases, including pine bark beetles, dogwood anthracnose, and sudden oak death.

Hargrave, R.; Johnson, G.R.; Zins, M.E. 2002. *Planting trees and shrubs for long-term health.* MI-07681-S. St. Paul, MN: University of Minnesota Extension Service.

An Illustrated Guide to Pruning (Gilman 2002)

International Society of Arboriculture: http://www.isa-arbor.com, including their *Tree City USA Bulletin* series

National Arbor Day Foundation: http://www.arborday.org

Native Trees, Shrubs, and Vines for Urban and Rural America (Hightshoe 1988)

North Carolina Cooperative Extension Service. http://www.ces. ncsu.edu/depts/hort/consumer/index.html. The website of the NCCES offers Plant Fact Sheets to help in choosing appropriate species, planting and care advice and information on urban integrated pest management.

Principles and Practice of Planting Trees and Shrubs (Watson and Himelick 1997)

Southeast Mississippi Resource Conservation & Development Council. 2006. *A Homeowner's Guide for Coastal Landscapes. Hurricane Resistant Landscapes. Preparing for the Storm.* Hattiesburg, MS: Southeast Mississippi Resource Conservation & Development Council

Training Young Trees for Structure and Form (Costello 2000) video

Tree City USA Bulletin series (Fazio, undated), International Society of Arboriculture (ISA) brochures (www.isa-arbor.com and www.treesaregood.com)

TreeLink: http://www.treelink.org *Trees for Urban and Suburban Landscapes* (Gilman 1997)

These suggested references are only a starting point. Your local cooperative extension agent or state forestry agency can provide you with up-to-date and local information.

Appendix B: Benefit–Cost Information Tables

Information in this Appendix can be used to estimate benefits and costs associated with proposed tree plantings. The tables contain data for representative large (*Quercus virginiana*, Southern live oak), medium (*Magnolia grandiflora*, Southern magnolia), and small (*Cornus florida*, dogwood) broadleaf trees and a representative conifer (*Pinus taeda*, loblolly pine). Data are presented as annual values for each 5-year interval after planting (*Tables 1–4*). Annual values incorporate effects of tree loss. Based on the results of our survey, we assume that 35% of the trees planted die by the end of the 40-year period.

The tables are divided into three sections: benefits, costs, and net benefits. For the benefits section of the tables, there are two columns for each 5-year interval. In the first column, values describe **resource units** (RUs): for example, the amount of air conditioning energy saved in kWh per year per tree, air pollutant uptake in pounds per year per tree, and rainfall intercepted in gallons per year per tree. Energy and CO_2 benefits for residential yard trees are broken out by tree location to show how shading impacts vary among trees opposite west-, south-, and east-facing building walls. The second column for each 5-year interval contains dollar values obtained by multiplying RUs by local prices (e.g., kWh saved [RU] x $/kWh).

In the second section of the tables, costs are broken down into categories for yard and public trees. Costs for yard trees do not vary by planting location (i.e., east, west, south walls). Although tree and planting costs occur at year one, we divided this value by five years to derive an average annual cost for the first 5-year period. All other costs are the estimated values for each year and not values averaged over five years.

In the third section of the tables, total net benefits are calculated by subtracting total costs from total benefits. Data are presented for a yard tree opposite west-, south-, and east-facing walls, as well as for the public tree.

The last column in each table presents 40-year-average annual values. These numbers were calculated by dividing the total costs and benefits by 40 years.

Table B1. Annual benefits, costs and net benefits at 5-year intervals for a representative large broadleaf tree (Southern live oak, Quercus virginiana*). The 40-year average is also shown.*

Benefits/tree	Year 5 RU	$	Year 10 RU	$	Year 15 RU	$	Year 20 RU	$	Year 25 RU	$	Year 30 RU	$	Year 35 RU	$	Year 40 RU	$	40 year average RU	$
Cooling (kWh)																		
Yard: west	89	8 32	221	20 61	309	28 85	386	36 01	431	40 28	466	43 49	484	45 16	470	43 91	357	33 33
Yard: south	54	5 05	147	13 70	216	20 13	283	26 41	325	30 36	358	33 46	377	35 20	383	35 76	268	25 01
Yard: east	97	9 03	230	21 52	319	29 78	394	36 82	439	40 97	468	43 72	482	45 02	466	43 55	362	33 80
Public	39	3 66	100	9 33	145	13 50	192	17 95	223	20 85	249	23 25	264	24 66	276	25 80	186	17 38
Heating (kBtu)																		
Yard: west	-25	-0 30	22	0 27	81	0 97	127	1 52	155	1 86	164	1 97	167	2 00	218	2 61	114	1 36
Yard: south	-181	-2 16	-550	-6 58	-740	-8 87	-857	-10 26	-912	-10 93	-941	-11 27	-946	-11 33	-774	-9 27	-738	-8 83
Yard: east	-68	-0 81	-18	-0 21	40	0 48	91	1 09	123	1 48	146	1 75	160	1 91	228	2 73	88	1 05
Public	145	1 73	341	4 08	467	5 59	563	6 74	616	7 37	648	7 76	661	7 91	664	7 95	513	6 14
Net energy (kBtu)																		
Yard: west	865	8 01	2,229	20 87	3,170	29 82	3,983	37 53	4,469	42 14	4,821	45 46	5,003	47 16	4,920	46 52	3,683	34 69
Yard: south	360	2 88	917	7 12	1,415	11 26	1,971	16 14	2,339	19 44	2,642	22 19	2,823	23 87	3,055	26 49	1,940	16 18
Yard: east	899	8 21	2,286	21 30	3,229	30 26	4,033	37 90	4,510	42 44	4,828	45 47	4,981	46 94	4,892	46 28	3,707	34 85
Public	537	5 39	1,340	13 41	1,912	19 09	2,485	24 69	2,848	28 22	3,137	31 01	3,302	32 57	3,427	33 76	2,373	23 52
Net CO$_2$ (lb)																		
Yard: west	176	1 32	427	3 21	595	4 46	732	5 50	817	6 13	871	6 54	900	6 75	889	6 67	676	5 07
Yard: south	110	0 82	259	1 94	371	2 78	476	3 57	546	4 10	594	4 46	623	4 67	653	4 89	454	3 41
Yard: east	181	1 36	436	3 27	604	4 53	741	5 55	823	6 17	873	6 54	897	6 73	885	6 63	680	5 10
Public	128	0 96	300	2 25	416	3 12	520	3 90	586	4 40	632	4 74	657	4 93	676	5 07	489	3 67
Air pollution (lb)																		
O$_3$ uptake	0 15	0 15	0 40	0 42	0 62	0 64	0 84	0 88	1 01	1 06	1 19	1 24	1 33	1 39	1 47	1 53	0 88	0 91
NO$_2$ uptake+avoided	0 21	0 22	0 53	0 55	0 76	0 79	0 98	1 02	1 12	1 16	1 23	1 28	1 30	1 35	1 32	1 38	0 93	0 97
SO$_2$ uptake+avoided	0 60	0 77	1 50	1 93	2 13	2 74	2 72	3 49	3 08	3 95	3 36	4 31	3 51	4 51	3 50	4 50	2 55	3 27
PM$_{10}$ uptake+avoided	0 05	0 04	0 16	0 12	0 31	0 24	0 52	0 39	0 72	0 54	0 91	0 69	1 10	0 84	1 27	0 97	0 63	0 48
VOCs avoided	0 05	0 07	0 12	0 17	0 16	0 24	0 21	0 31	0 24	0 35	0 26	0 38	0 27	0 40	0 27	0 40	0 20	0 29
BVOCs released	-0 06	-0 09	-0 28	-0 41	-0 82	-1 21	-1 95	-2 89	-3 55	-5 26	-5 61	-8 32	-8 15	-12 08	-11 15	-16 53	-3 95	-5 85
Avoided + net uptake	0 98	1 15	2 43	2 78	3 17	3 44	3 32	3 20	2 62	1 81	1 33	-0 42	-0 64	-3 60	-3 32	-7 76	1 24	0 08
Hydrology (gal)																		
Rainfall interception	836	5 06	2,309	13 97	3,644	22 05	5,226	31 62	6,460	39 08	7,862	47 57	9,020	54 57	10,235	61 92	5,699	34 48
Aesthetics and other benefits																		
Yard		1 19		22 49		38 90		52 77		64 24		73 47		80 60		85 79		52 43
Public		1 33		25 12		43 45		58 94		71 75		82 06		90 03		95 82		58 56
Total benefits																		
Yard: west		16 73		63 32		98 67		130 62		153 40		172 61		185 49		193 13		126 75
Yard: south		11 10		48 30		78 43		107 30		128 67		147 26		160 12		171 34		106 57
Yard: east		16 97		63 81		99 18		131 04		153 75		172 63		185 24		192 87		126 94
Public		13 89		57 53		91 14		122 34		145 26		164 95		178 50		188 81		120 30
Costs ($/year/tree)																		
Tree & planting																		
Yard		40 00																5 00
Public		30 00																3 75
Pruning																		
Yard		0 19		5 50		5 26		5 01		4 77		15 3		14 48		13 65		7 63
Public		4 63		6 64		6 35		6 05		5 76		20 04		18 96		17 88		10 27
Remove and dispose																		
Yard		3 98		3 58		4 79		5 82		6 72		7 51		8 24		8 90		5 62
Public		2 49		2 24		3 00		3 64		4 20		4 70		5 15		5 56		3 55
Pest & disease																		
Yard		0 30		0 50		0 64		0 74		0 81		0 86		0 89		0 91		0 67
Public		0 00		0 00		0 00		0 00		0 00		0 00		0 00		0 00		0 00
Infrastructure repair																		
Yard		0 10		0 17		0 21		0 25		0 27		0 29		0 30		0 30		0 22
Public		1 02		1 67		2 14		2 47		2 71		2 88		2 99		3 05		2 23
Clean-Up																		
Yard		0 05		0 08		0 10		0 11		0 13		0 13		0 14		0 14		0 10
Public		0 47		0 78		0 10		1 15		1 27		1 35		1 39		1 42		1 04
Admin/Inspect/Other																		
Yard		0 00		0 00		0 00		0 00		0 00		0 00		0 00		0 00		0 00
Public		0 81		1 34		1 71		1 98		2 17		2 31		2 39		2 44		1 78
Total costs																		
Yard		44 62		9 82		11 00		11 93		12 69		24 10		24 04		23 90		19 24
Public		39 41		12 66		14 18		15 30		16 11		31 27		30 88		30 34		23 24
Total net benefits																		
Yard: west		-27 89		53 50		87 67		118 68		140 71		148 51		161 44		169 23		107 50
Yard: south		-33 52		38 48		67 44		95 37		115 98		123 17		136 07		147 43		87 32
Yard: east		-27 65		53 99		88 18		119 11		141 06		148 53		161 20		168 96		107 69
Public		-25 53		44 86		76 96		107 04		129 15		133 69		147 63		158 47		97 07

Table B2. Annual benefits, costs and net benefits at 5-year intervals for a representative medium broadleaf tree (Southern magnolia, Magnolia grandiflora*). The 40-year average is also shown.*

	Year 5		Year 10		Year 15		Year 20		Year 25		Year 30		Year 35		Year 40		40 year average	
Benefits/tree	RU	$	RU	$	RU	$	RU	$	RU	$	RU	$	RU	$	RU	$	RU	$
Cooling (kWh)																		
Yard: west	14	1 33	49	4 55	94	8 80	135	12 59	169	15 77	197	18 41	216	20 21	232	21 70	138	12 92
Yard: south	8	0 77	28	2 65	56	5 20	83	7 77	108	10 06	130	12 12	148	13 84	164	15 30	91	8 46
Yard: east	18	1 65	57	5 28	102	9 56	142	13 21	174	16 20	200	18 69	219	20 41	234	21 83	143	13 36
Public	7	0 67	22	2 01	38	3 58	53	5 12	69	6 48	83	7 73	95	8 85	105	9 81	59	5 53
Heating (kBtu)																		
Yard: west	-4	-0 04	-22	-0 27	-40	-0 48	-29	-0 34	-7	-0 08	18	0 21	47	0 56	72	0 87	4	0 05
Yard: south	-8	-0 10	-85	-1 02	-230	-2 75	-350	-4 19	-447	-5 35	-512	-6 13	-527	-6 31	-537	-6 43	-337	-4 03
Yard: east	-23	-0 28	-65	-0 78	-86	-1 03	-70	-0 84	-41	-0 49	-10	-0 12	25	0 30	57	0 68	-27	-0 32
Public	29	0 35	83	0 99	144	1 73	201	2 41	250	2 99	291	3 48	320	3 83	344	4 12	208	2 49
Net energy (kBtu)																		
Yard: west	138	1 28	465	4 28	902	8 32	1,319	12 25	1,682	15 69	1,989	18 62	2,210	20 77	2,396	22 56	1,388	12 97
Yard: south	74	0 67	199	1 63	327	2 45	482	3 58	631	4 71	785	5 98	955	7 54	1,102	8 88	570	4 43
Yard: east	153	1 37	501	4 51	938	8 53	1,345	12 37	1,694	15 72	1,992	18 57	2,211	20 72	2,394	22 51	1,404	13 04
Public	101	1 02	298	3 01	528	5 31	749	7 53	943	9 47	1,118	11 21	1,268	12 69	1,394	13 93	800	8 02
Net CO$_2$ (lb)																		
Yard: west	22	0 17	76	0 57	147	1 11	217	1 63	280	2 10	334	2 51	376	2 82	413	3 10	234	1 75
Yard: south	14	0 10	41	0 31	72	0 54	109	0 82	145	1 08	180	1 35	216	1 62	248	1 86	129	0 96
Yard: east	25	0 19	82	0 62	153	1 15	222	1 66	282	2 12	336	2 52	377	2 83	414	3 10	237	1 77
Public	17	0 13	52	0 39	93	0 69	135	1 01	174	1 30	210	1 58	242	1 82	271	2 03	149	1 12
Air pollution (lb)																		
O$_3$ uptake	0 03	0 03	0 09	0 09	0 16	0 17	0 24	0 25	0 33	0 34	0 41	0 43	0 49	0 52	0 58	0 60	0 29	0 30
NO$_2$ uptake+avoided	0 04	0 04	0 12	0 12	0 21	0 22	0 31	0 32	0 39	0 41	0 47	0 49	0 53	0 55	0 59	0 61	0 33	0 35
SO$_2$ uptake+avoided	0 10	0 13	0 33	0 43	0 63	0 80	0 89	1 15	1 12	1 44	1 32	1 70	1 47	1 89	1 60	2 06	0 93	1 20
PM$_{10}$ uptake+avoided	0 01	0 01	0 05	0 04	0 13	0 10	0 25	0 19	0 36	0 27	0 47	0 36	0 58	0 44	0 59	0 45	0 31	0 23
VOCs avoided	0 01	0 01	0 03	0 04	0 05	0 07	0 07	0 10	0 09	0 13	0 10	0 15	0 11	0 17	0 12	0 18	0 07	0 11
BVOCs released	-0 06	-0 10	-0 21	-0 31	-0 46	-0 69	-0 88	-1 30	-1 37	-2 03	-1 94	-2 88	-2 60	-3 86	-2 60	-3 86	-1 27	-1 88
Avoided + net uptake	0 12	0 12	0 40	0 41	0 72	0 68	0 89	0 71	0 92	0 57	0 83	0 24	0 59	-0 29	0 88	0 04	0 67	0 31
Hydrology (gal)																		
Rainfall interception	256	1 55	659	3 98	1,124	6 80	1,646	9 96	2,173	13 14	2,719	16 45	3,281	19 85	3,842	23 25	1,962	11 87
Aesthetics and other benefits																		
Yard		12 49		12 97		13 48		13 80		13 96		13 96		13 81		13 54		13 50
Public		13 95		14 49		15 05		15 42		15 59		15 59		15 43		15 12		15 08
Total benefits																		
Yard: west		15 61		22 22		30 38		38 35		45 46		51 78		56 96		62 49		40 41
Yard: south		14 94		19 30		23 94		28 87		33 47		37 98		42 53		47 57		31 08
Yard: east		15 72		22 48		30 64		38 51		45 50		51 74		56 92		62 44		40 49
Public		16 76		22 27		28 53		34 63		40 07		45 07		49 49		54 38		36 40
Costs ($/year/tree)																		
Tree & planting																		
Yard		40 00																5 00
Public		30 00																3 75
Pruning																		
Yard		0 19		0 29		5 26		5 01		4 77		4 52		14 48		13 65		5 62
Public		4 63		3 32		6 35		6 05		5 76		5 46		18 96		17 88		8 03
Remove and dispose																		
Yard		2 00		1 90		2 73		3 55		4 34		5 12		5 88		6 62		3 59
Public		1 25		1 19		1 71		2 22		2 71		3 20		3 67		4 14		2 27
Pest & disease																		
Yard		0 15		0 26		0 36		0 45		0 52		0 59		0 64		0 68		0 43
Public		0 00		0 00		0 00		0 00		0 00		0 00		0 00		0 00		0 00
Infrastructure repair																		
Yard		0 05		0 09		0 12		0 15		0 17		0 20		0 18		0 23		0 14
Public		0 51		0 89		1 22		1 51		1 76		1 96		2 13		2 27		1 42
Clean-Up																		
Yard		0 02		0 04		0 06		0 07		0 08		0 09		0 09		0 11		0 07
Public		0 24		0 41		0 57		0 70		0 82		0 92		0 10		1 06		0 66
Admin/Inspect/Other																		
Yard		0 00		0 00		0 00		0 00		0 00		0 00		0 00		0 00		0 00
Public		0 41		0 71		0 97		1 21		1 40		1 57		1 71		1 81		1 14
Total costs																		
Yard		42 42		2 58		8 53		9 23		9 89		10 52		21 26		21 28		14 84
Public		37 03		6 51		10 82		11 69		12 45		13 12		27 47		27 15		17 89
Total net benefits																		
Yard: west		-26 80		19 64		21 85		29 12		35 57		41 26		35 70		41 22		25 56
Yard: south		-27 48		16 72		15 41		19 64		23 57		27 46		21 27		26 29		16 23
Yard: east		-26 69		19 90		22 11		29 28		35 61		41 22		35 66		41 16		25 65

Table B3. Annual benefits, costs and net benefits at 5-year intervals for a representative small broadleaf tree (dogwood, Cornus florida). The 40-year average is also shown.

Benefits/tree	Year 5 RU	$	Year 10 RU	$	Year 15 RU	$	Year 20 RU	$	Year 25 RU	$	Year 30 RU	$	Year 35 RU	$	Year 40 RU	$	40 year average RU	$
Cooling (kWh)																		
Yard: west	32	2 96	63	5 90	83	7 73	100	9 38	109	10 20	116	10 82	119	11 08	121	11 25	93	8 67
Yard: south	18	1 67	36	3 38	49	4 56	60	5 62	66	6 14	70	6 53	72	6 69	73	6 80	55	5 17
Yard: east	36	3 37	71	6 62	92	8 61	111	10 39	120	11 23	126	11 81	129	12 03	130	12 15	102	9 52
Public	16	1 54	32	3 02	43	3 99	52	4 85	56	5 26	59	5 54	61	5 65	61	5 72	48	4 45
Heating (kBtu)																		
Yard: west	36	0 43	66	0 79	86	1 03	105	1 25	114	1 37	122	1 46	125	1 49	127	1 52	98	1 17
Yard: south	31	0 37	44	0 53	48	0 58	51	0 62	51	0 61	48	0 58	46	0 55	43	0 52	45	0 54
Yard: east	23	0 28	47	0 56	66	0 79	83	0 99	92	1 10	100	1 20	104	1 25	107	1 28	78	0 93
Public	66	0 79	123	1 48	157	1 88	188	2 25	202	2 42	212	2 54	215	2 58	217	2 60	173	2 07
Net energy (kBtu)																		
Yard: west	353	3 39	697	6 68	915	8 77	1,109	10 64	1,206	11 56	1,280	12 27	1,311	12 58	1,332	12 77	1,025	9 83
Yard: south	210	2 04	407	3 91	537	5 14	653	6 23	708	6 75	747	7 11	763	7 24	772	7 33	600	5 72
Yard: east	384	3 64	755	7 18	987	9 39	1,195	11 38	1,294	12 33	1,364	13 00	1,392	13 27	1,408	13 44	1,097	10 45
Public	231	2 33	447	4 50	584	5 87	707	7 10	765	7 68	805	8 08	821	8 23	830	8 32	649	6 51
Net CO$_2$ (lb)																		
Yard: west	58	0 44	111	0 83	142	1 07	170	1 28	183	1 37	192	1 44	195	1 46	197	1 47	160	1 17
Yard: south	39	0 29	72	0 54	91	0 68	109	0 81	116	0 87	120	0 90	121	0 91	122	0 91	99	0 74
Yard: east	63	0 47	119	0 90	152	1 14	182	1 37	196	1 47	204	1 53	206	1 55	208	1 56	166	1 25
Public	41	0 31	76	0 57	96	0 72	113	0 85	121	0 91	125	0 94	126	0 95	126	0 95	103	0 77
Air pollution (lb)																		
O$_3$ uptake	0 05	0 05	0 10	0 11	0 14	0 14	0 17	0 18	0 20	0 21	0 22	0 23	0 24	0 25	0 26	0 27	0 17	0 18
NO$_2$ uptake+avoided	0 08	0 08	0 15	0 16	0 20	0 21	0 24	0 25	0 26	0 28	0 28	0 29	0 29	0 30	0 29	0 31	0 22	0 23
SO$_2$ uptake+avoided	0 22	0 28	0 43	0 55	0 56	0 72	0 69	0 88	0 74	0 96	0 79	1 01	0 81	1 03	0 82	1 05	0 63	0 81
PM$_{10}$ uptake+avoided	0 02	0 02	0 06	0 05	0 11	0 09	0 17	0 13	0 18	0 13	0 18	0 14	0 18	0 14	0 18	0 14	0 14	0 10
VOCs avoided	0 02	0 03	0 03	0 05	0 04	0 07	0 05	0 08	0 06	0 09	0 06	0 09	0 06	0 09	0 06	0 10	0 05	0 07
BVOCs released	0	0	0	0	0	0	0	0	0	0	0	0	0	0	0	0	0	0
Avoided + net uptake	0 38	0 45	0 78	0 91	1 06	1 23	1 33	1 53	1 45	1 66	1 54	1 77	1 58	1 82	1 62	1 86	1 22	1 40
Hydrology (gal)																		
Rainfall interception	209	1 26	418	2 53	569	3 44	720	4 36	826	4 99	931	5 63	1,014	6 13	1,097	6 63	723	4 37
Aesthetics and other benefits																		
Yard		2 53		1 89		1 54		1 29		1 11		0 96		0 85		0 75		1 36
Public		2 83		2 11		1 72		1 44		1 24		1 08		0 94		0 83		1 52
Total benefits																		
Yard: west		8 07		12 85		16 04		19 09		20 70		22 08		22 84		23 49		18 15
Yard: south		6 58		9 79		12 03		14 22		15 39		16 37		16 96		17 48		13 60
Yard: east		8 36		13 41		16 74		19 92		21 56		22 90		23 62		24 24		18 84
Public		7 18		10 62		12 97		15 28		16 48		17 49		18 08		18 60		14 59
Costs ($/year/tree)																		
Tree & planting																		
Yard		40 00																5 00
Public		30 00																3 75
Pruning																		
Yard		0 19		0 29		5 26		5 01		4 77		4 52		4 28		4 04		3 49
Public		4 63		3 32		6 35		6 05		5 76		5 46		5 17		4 88		5 23
Remove and dispose																		
Yard		2 24		1 83		2 33		2 73		3 07		3 36		3 63		3 86		2 61
Public		1 40		1 14		1 45		1 70		1 92		2 10		2 27		2 41		1 65
Pest & disease																		
Yard		0 17		0 26		0 31		0 35		0 37		0 39		0 39		0 40		0 31
Public		0 00		0 00		0 00		0 00		0 00		0 00		0 00		0 00		0 00
Infrastructure repair																		
Yard		0 06		0 09		0 10		0 12		0 12		0 13		0 13		0 13		0 10
Public		0 57		0 85		1 04		1 16		1 24		1 29		1 32		1 32		1 04
Clean-up																		
Yard		0 03		0 04		0 05		0 05		0 06		0 06		0 06		0 06		0 05
Public		0 27		0 40		0 48		0 54		0 58		0 60		0 61		0 62		0 49
Admin/Inspect/Other																		
Yard		0 00		0 00		0 00		0 00		0 00		0 00		0 00		0 00		0 00
Public		0 46		0 68		0 83		0 93		0 99		1 03		1 05		1 06		0 84
Total costs																		
Yard		42 68		2 50		8 04		8 26		8 39		8 46		8 49		8 49		11 56
Public		37 32		6 40		10 15		10 39		10 49		10 49		10 42		10 29		13 62
Total net benefits																		
Yard: west		-34 61		10 36		8 00		10 83		12 32		13 62		14 35		15 01		6 58
Yard: south		-36 11		7 29		3 99		5 97		7 00		7 91		8 46		8 99		2 04
Yard: east		-34 32		10 91		8 70		11 66		13 17		14 44		15 13		15 75		7 28
Public		-30 14		4 22		2 82		4 89		5 99		7 00		7 66		8 31		0 97

Table B4. Annual benefits, costs and net benefits at 5-year intervals for a representative conifer (loblolly pine, Pinus taeda*). The 40-year average is also shown.*

Benefits/tree	Year 5 RU	Year 5 $	Year 10 RU	Year 10 $	Year 15 RU	Year 15 $	Year 20 RU	Year 20 $	Year 25 RU	Year 25 $	Year 30 RU	Year 30 $	Year 35 RU	Year 35 $	Year 40 RU	Year 40 $	40 year average RU	40 year average $
Cooling (kWh)																		
Yard: west	22	2 10	94	8 81	160	14 93	213	19 92	249	23 28	277	25 88	297	27 70	312	29 17	203	18 97
Yard: south	12	1 09	57	5 32	106	9 91	152	14 23	186	17 39	215	20 06	236	22 04	254	23 71	152	14 22
Yard: east	24	2 25	96	8 99	160	14 90	209	19 49	244	22 81	274	25 60	293	27 35	307	28 64	201	18 76
Public	7	0 64	32	3 03	61	5 70	89	8 31	112	10 46	134	12 48	151	14 13	167	15 62	94	8 80
Heating (kBtu)																		
Yard: west	-23	-0 28	-36	-0 43	22	0 26	103	1 23	165	1 98	220	2 64	258	3 08	287	3 44	125	1 49
Yard: south	-66	-0 79	-306	-3 67	-468	-5 60	-481	-5 76	-459	-5 50	-416	-4 98	-374	-4 47	-331	-3 97	-363	-4 34
Yard: east	-36	-0 44	-48	-0 57	26	0 31	119	1 42	187	2 24	245	2 93	283	3 39	312	3 74	136	1 63
Public	29	0 35	121	1 45	219	2 63	311	3 72	374	4 48	426	5 10	459	5 48	481	5 75	302	3 62
Net energy (kBtu)																		
Yard: west	201	1 82	908	8 39	1,620	15 19	2,236	21 15	2,658	25 26	2,991	28 51	3,223	30 78	3,411	32 61	2,156	20 46
Yard: south	50	0 30	264	1 66	593	4 31	1,042	8 47	1,403	11 89	1,731	15 08	1,986	17 56	2,207	19 74	1,160	9 87
Yard: east	205	1 82	915	8 42	1,622	15 21	2,206	20 91	2,630	25 06	2,986	28 53	3,212	30 74	3,379	32 38	2,144	20 38
Public	98	0 99	446	4 49	830	8 33	1,200	12 03	1,495	14 95	1,762	17 58	1,971	19 61	2,154	21 38	1,244	12 42
Net CO_2 (lb)																		
Yard: west	32	0 24	149	1 12	271	2 03	382	2 87	462	3 46	527	3 95	575	4 32	618	4 63	377	2 83
Yard: south	12	0 09	66	0 50	140	1 05	230	1 73	302	2 26	367	2 75	418	3 14	465	3 49	250	1 88
Yard: east	33	0 25	150	1 13	271	2 03	378	2 84	457	3 43	526	3 94	573	4 30	613	4 60	375	2 81
Public	17	0 13	83	0 62	160	1 19	237	1 78	299	2 24	355	2 66	400	3 00	442	3 31	249	1 87
Air pollution (lb)																		
O_3 uptake	0 03	0 03	0 13	0 13	0 25	0 27	0 40	0 41	0 53	0 55	0 66	0 69	0 78	0 81	0 90	0 94	0 46	0 48
NO_2 uptake+avoided	0 05	0 05	0 20	0 21	0 36	0 38	0 51	0 53	0 62	0 65	0 72	0 75	0 80	0 83	0 87	0 90	0 52	0 54
SO_2 uptake+avoided	0 14	0 18	0 60	0 77	1 05	1 34	1 43	1 84	1 71	2 20	1 96	2 51	2 13	2 73	2 28	2 92	1 41	1 81
PM_{10} uptake+avoided	0 01	0 01	0 08	0 06	0 18	0 14	0 32	0 24	0 46	0 35	0 60	0 45	0 73	0 56	0 86	0 65	0 41	0 31
VOCs avoided	0 01	0 02	0 05	0 07	0 08	0 12	0 11	0 16	0 13	0 20	0 15	0 22	0 16	0 24	0 17	0 26	0 11	0 16
BVOCs released	-0 01	-0 02	-0 02	-0 02	-0 40	-0 60	-1 50	-2 22	-3 26	-4 83	-5 68	-8 41	-8 76	-12 98	-12 50	-18 53	-4 01	-5 95
Avoided + net uptake	0 23	0 27	1 04	1 22	1 52	1 64	1 27	0 97	0 20	-0 88	-1 59	-3 78	-4 15	-7 80	-7 42	-12 85	-1 11	-2 65
Hydrology (gal)																		
Rainfall interception	86	0 52	507	3 07	1,185	7 17	2,098	12 70	3,048	18 44	4,112	24 88	5,177	31 32	6,313	38 19	2,816	17 04
Aesthetics and other benefits																		
Yard		1 10		13 11		21 03		26 48		30 09		32 34		33 57		34 03		23 97
Public		1 23		14 65		23 49		29 57		33 61		36 12		37 50		38 01		26 77
Total benefits																		
Yard: west		3 95		26 91		47 06		64 17		76 37		85 90		92 19		96 61		61 64
Yard: south		2 28		19 55		35 20		50 34		61 81		71 26		77 79		82 59		50 10
Yard: east		3 95		26 95		47 09		63 89		76 14		85 91		92 14		96 34		61 55
Public		3 14		24 04		41 82		57 04		68 35		77 46		83 63		88 04		55 44
Costs ($/year/tree)																		
Tree & planting																		
Yard		40 00																5 00
Public		30 00																3 75
Pruning																		
Yard		0 19		0 29		0 27		0 26		0 25		0 24		0 22		0 21		0 25
Public		4 63		3 32		3 17		3 03		2 88		2 73		2 58		2 44		3 17
Remove & dispose																		
Yard		3 98		2 26		3 41		4 49		5 50		6 45		7 35		8 20		4 45
Public		2 49		1 41		2 13		2 81		3 44		4 03		4 59		5 13		2 80
Pest & disease																		
Yard		0 30		0 31		0 45		0 57		0 66		0 74		0 80		0 84		0 53
Public		0 00		0 00		0 00		0 00		0 00		0 00		0 00		0 00		0 00
Infrastructure repair																		
Yard		0 10		0 10		0 15		0 19		0 22		0 25		0 27		0 28		0 18
Public		1 02		1 05		1 52		1 91		2 22		2 47		2 67		2 81		1 76
Clean-up																		
Yard		0 05		0 05		0 07		0 09		0 10		0 12		0 12		0 13		0 08
Public		0 47		0 49		0 71		0 89		1 04		1 15		1 24		1 31		0 82
Admin/Inspect/Other																		
Yard		0 00		0 00		0 00		0 00		0 00		0 00		0 00		0 00		0 00
Public		0 81		0 41		1 22		1 53		1 78		1 98		2 13		2 25		1 41
Total costs																		
Yard		44 62		3 01		4 36		5 60		6 74		7 79		8 76		9 66		10 48
Public		39 41		6 68		8 75		10 16		11 36		12 37		13 22		13 93		14 31
Total net benefits																		
Yard: west		-40 67		23 89		42 71		58 57		69 63		78 11		83 43		86 94		51 17
Yard: south		-42 34		16 54		30 84		44 74		55 07		63 48		69 03		72 93		39 63
Yard: east		-40 67		23 94		42 73		58 29		69 40		78 13		83 38		86 67		51 07
Public		-36 28		17 36		33 07		46 89		57 00		65 08		70 41		74 11		41 13

Appendix C: Procedures for Estimating Benefits and Costs

Approach

Pricing Benefits and Costs

Public and private trees in different locations

In this study, annual benefits and costs over a 40-year planning horizon were estimated for newly planted trees in three residential yard locations (east, south, and west of the dwelling unit) and a public streetside or park location. Trees in these hypothetical locations are called "yard" and "public" trees, respectively. Prices were assigned to each cost (e.g. planting, pruning, removal, irrigation, infrastructure repair, liability) and benefit (e.g., heating/cooling, energy savings, air-pollution reduction, stormwater-runoff reduction) through direct estimation and implied valuation of benefits as environmental externalities. This approach made it possible to estimate the net benefits of plantings in "typical" locations with "typical" tree species.

To account for differences in the mature size and growth rates of different tree species, we report results for a large (*Quercus virginiana*, Southern live oak), medium (*Magnolia grandiflora*, Southern magnolia), and small (*Cornus florida*, flowering dogwood) broadleaf tree and for a conifer (*Pinus taeda*, loblolly pine). Results are reported for 5-year intervals for 40 years.

Mature tree height and leaf surface area are useful indicators

Mature tree height is frequently used to characterize large, medium, and small species because matching tree height to available overhead space is an important design consideration. However, in this analysis, leaf surface area (LSA) and crown diameter were also used to characterize **mature tree size**. These additional measurements are useful indicators for many functional benefits of trees that relate to leaf–atmosphere processes (e.g., interception, transpiration, photosynthesis). Tree growth rates, dimensions, and LSA estimates are based on tree growth modeling.

Growth Modeling

Growth models are based on data collected in Charleston, SC. An inventory of Charleston's street trees was provided by the city's Urban Forestry Division staff. Initially conducted in 1992, the inventory was updated annually through 2004 and included 15,244 trees.

Tree-growth models developed from Charleston data were used as the basis for modeling tree growth for this report. Using Charleston's tree inventory, we measured a stratified random sample of 19 tree species to establish relations between tree age, size, leaf area and biomass.

For the growth models, information spanning the life cycle of pre-dominant tree species was collected. The inventory was stratified into the following nine diameter-at-breast-height (DBH) classes:

- 0–3 in (0–7.6 cm)
- 3–6 in (7.6–15.2 cm)
- 6–12 in (15.2–30.5 cm)
- 12–18 in (30.5–45.7 cm)
- 18–24 in (45.7–61.0 cm)
- 24–30 in (61.0–76.2 cm)
- 30–36 in (76.2–91.4 cm)
- 36–42 in (91.4–106.7 cm)
- >42 in (106.7 cm)

Thirty to seventy trees of each species were randomly selected for surveying, along with an equal number of alternative trees. Tree measurements included DBH (to nearest 0.1 cm by sonar measuring device), tree crown and bole height (to nearest 0.5 m by clinometer), crown diameter in two directions (parallel and perpendicular to nearest street to nearest 0.5 m by sonar measuring device), tree condition and location. Replacement trees were sampled when trees from the original sample population could not be located. Tree age was determined by street-tree managers. Fieldwork was conducted in September 2004.

Crown volume and leaf area were estimated from computer processing of tree-crown images obtained using a digital camera. The method has shown greater accuracy than other techniques (±20% of actual leaf area) in estimating crown volume and leaf area of open-grown trees (Peper and McPherson 2003).

Linear regression was used to fit predictive models with DBH as a function of age for each of the 19 sampled species. Predictions of leaf surface area (LSA), crown diameter, and height metrics were modeled as a function of DBH using best-fit models. After inspecting the growth curves for each species, we selected the typical large, medium, and small tree species for this report.

Reporting Results

Results are reported in terms of annual values per tree planted. However, to make these calculations realistic, mortality rates are included. Based on our survey of regional municipal foresters and commercial arborists, this analysis assumed that 35% of the hypothetical planted trees died over the 40-year period. Annual mortality rates were 1.5% for the first 5 years, and 0.80% per year after that, or 35% total. This accounting approach "grows" trees in different locations and uses

Annual values reported

computer simulation to directly calculate the annual flow of benefits and costs as trees mature and die (McPherson 1992).

Benefits and costs are connected with size of tree

Benefits and costs are directly connected with tree-size variables such as trunk DBH, tree canopy cover, and LSA. For instance, pruning and removal costs usually increase with tree size, expressed as DBH. For some parameters, such as sidewalk repair, costs are negligible for young trees but increase relatively rapidly as tree roots grow large enough to heave pavement. For other parameters, such as air-pollutant uptake and rainfall interception, benefits are related to tree canopy cover and leaf area.

Annual vs. periodic costs

Most benefits occur on an annual basis, but some costs are periodic. For instance, street trees may be pruned on regular cycles but are removed in a less regular fashion (e.g., when they pose a hazard or soon after they die). In this analysis, most costs and benefits are reported for the year in which they occur. However, periodic costs such as pruning, pest and disease control, and infrastructure repair are presented on an average annual basis. Although spreading one-time costs over each year of a maintenance cycle does not alter the 40-year nominal expenditure, it can lead to inaccuracies if future costs are discounted to the present.

Benefit and Cost Valuation

Source of cost estimates

Source of cost estimates

Frequency and costs of tree management were estimated based on surveys with municipal foresters from Jacksonville, FL; Savannah, GA; and Charleston, SC. In addition, commercial arborists in Houston, TX; Summerville, SC; and coastal GA provided information on tree management costs on residential properties.

Pricing benefits

Pricing benefits

To monetize effects of trees on energy use we take the perspective of a residential customer by using retail electricity and natural-gas prices for utilities serving Charleston. The retail price of energy reflects a full accounting of costs as paid by the end user, such as the utility costs of power generation, transmission, distribution, administration, marketing and profit. This perspective aligns with our modeling method, which calculates energy effects of trees based on differences among consumers in heating and air conditioning equipment types, saturations, building construction types, and base loads.

The preferred way to value air quality benefits from trees is to first determine the costs of damages to human health from polluted air, then calculate the value of avoided costs because trees are cleaning the air. Economic valuation of damages to human health usually uses information on willingness to pay to avoid damages obtained via interviews or direct estimates of the monetary costs of damages (e.g., alleviating headaches, extending life). Empirical correlations developed by Wang and Santini (1995) reviewed five studies and 15 sets of regional cost data to relate per-ton costs of various pollutant emissions to regional ambient air quality measurements and population size. We use their damaged-based estimates unless the values are negative, in which case we use their control-cost based estimates.

Calculating Benefits

Calculating Energy Benefits

The prototypical building used as a basis for the simulations was typical of post-1980 construction practices, and represents approximately one-third of the total single-family residential housing stock in the Coastal Plain region. The house was a one-story, wood-frame, slab-on-grade building with a conditioned floor area of 1,620 ft² (151 m²), window area (double-glazed) of 214 ft² (20 m²), and wall and ceiling insulation of R11 and R19, respectively. The central cooling system had a **seasonal energy efficiency ratio** (SEER) of 10, and the natural-gas furnace had an **annual fuel utilization efficiency (AFUE)** of 78%. Building footprints were square, reflecting average impacts for a large number of buildings (McPherson and Simpson 1999). Buildings were simulated with 1.5-ft (0.45-m) overhangs. Blinds had a visual density of 37% and were assumed to be closed when the air conditioner was operating. Summer thermostat settings were 78°F (25°C); winter settings were 68°F (20°C) during the day and 60°F (16°C) at night. Because the prototype building was larger, but more energy efficient, than most other construction types, our projected energy savings can be considered similar to those for older, less thermally efficient, but smaller buildings. The energy simulations relied on typical meteorological data from Charleston (Marion and Urban 1995).

Using a typical single family residence for energy simulations

Calculating energy savings

The dollar value of energy savings was based on regional average residential electricity and natural-gas prices of $0.093/**kWh** and $1.197/**therm**, respectively. Electricity and natural-gas prices were for 2005 for South Carolina (SCANA Corporation, 2005a and 2005b, respectively). Homes were assumed to have central air conditioning and natural-gas heating.

Calculating shade effects

Residential yard trees were within 60 ft (18 m) of homes so as to directly shade walls and windows. Shade effects of these trees on building energy use were simulated for large, medium, and small trees at three tree-to-building distances, following methods outlined by McPherson and Simpson (1999). The large tree (live oak) had a year-round visual density of 85%, the medium tree (Southern magnolia) 79%, and the conifer (loblolly pine) 85%. The small tree (dogwood) had visual densities of 75% during summer and 30% during winter. Leaf-off values for use in calculating winter shade were based on published values where available (McPherson 1984; Hammond et al. 1980). Foliation periods for deciduous trees were obtained from the literature (McPherson 1984; Hammond et al.1980) and adjusted for Charleston's climate based on consultation with forestry supervisors (Burbage 2005).

Large and medium broadleaf trees and conifers were evergreen, and small trees were leafless from October 15-April 15 (Burbage 2005). Results of shade effects for each tree were averaged over distance and weighted by occurrence within each of three distance classes: 28% at 10–20 ft (3–6 m), 68% at 20–40 ft (6–12 m), and 4% at 40–60 ft (12–18 m) (McPherson and Simpson 1999). Results are reported for trees shading east-, south-, and west-facing surfaces. Our results for public trees are conservative in that we assumed that they do not provide shading benefits. For example, in Modesto, CA, 15% of total annual dollar energy savings from street trees was due to shade and 85% due to **climate effects** (McPherson et al. 1999a).

Calculating climate effects

In addition to localized shade effects, which were assumed to accrue only to residential yard trees, lowered air temperatures and wind speeds from increased neighborhood tree cover (referred to as climate effects) produced a net decrease in demand for winter heating and summer cooling (reduced wind speeds by themselves may increase or decrease cooling demand, depending on the circumstances). Climate effects on energy use, air temperature and wind speed, as a function of neighborhood canopy cover, were estimated from published values (McPherson and Simpson 1999). Existing tree canopy plus building cover was 50% based on estimates for Miami and Dallas (McPherson and Simpson 1999). Canopy cover was calculated to increase by 1.0%, 1.2%, 2.1%, and 1.9% for 20-year-old large, medium, and small broadleaf and coniferous trees, respectively, based on an effective lot size (actual lot size plus a portion of adjacent street and other rights-of-way) of 10,000 ft² (929 m²), and one tree on average was assumed per lot. Climate effects were estimated by simulating effects of wind and air-temperature reductions on energy use. Climate effects accrued for both public and yard trees.

Calculating windbreak effects

Trees near buildings result in additional wind-speed reductions beyond those from the aggregate effects of trees throughout the neighborhood. This leads to a small additional reduction in annual heating energy use of about 0.4% per tree for this region (McPherson and Simpson 1999). Yard and public conifer trees were assumed to be windbreaks, and therefore located where they did not increase heating loads by obstructing winter sun. Windbreak effects were not attributed to broadleaf trees, since their crowns are leafless and above the ground, and therefore do not block winds near ground level.

Atmospheric Carbon Dioxide Reduction

Calculating reduction in CO_2 emissions from power plants

Conserving energy in buildings can reduce CO_2 emissions from power plants. These avoided emissions were calculated as the product of energy savings for heating and cooling using CO_2 **emission factors** (*Table C1*) based on data for SCANA where the average fuel mix is 0.3% oil, 0.4% natural gas, 66.5% coal, and 32.9% nuclear (US EPA 2003). The value of $15/ton CO_2 reduction (*Table C1*) was based on the average of high and low estimates by CO2e.com (2005).

Calculating carbon storage

Sequestration, the net rate of CO_2 storage in above- and belowground biomass over the course of one growing season, was calculated using tree height and DBH data with biomass equations (Pillsbury et al. 1998). Volume estimates were converted to green and dry-weight estimates (Markwardt 1930) and divided by 78% to incorporate root biomass. Dry-weight biomass was converted to carbon (50%) and these values were converted to CO_2. The amount of CO_2 sequestered each year is the annual increment of CO_2 stored as trees increase their biomass.

Calculating CO_2 released by power equipment

Tree-related emissions of CO_2, based on gasoline and diesel fuel consumption during tree care in our survey cities, were calculated using the value 0.34 lb CO_2/in DBH (0.061 kg CO_2 per cm DBH). This amount may overestimate CO_2 release associated with less intensively maintained residential yard trees.

Calculating CO_2 released during decomposition

To calculate CO_2 released through decomposition of dead woody biomass, we conservatively estimated that dead trees were removed and mulched in the year that death occurred, and that 80% of their

Table C1. Emissions factors and implied value of benefits for CO_2 and critical air pollutants.

	Emission Factor		
	Electricity (lb/MWh)[a]	Natural gas (lb/MBtu)[b]	Implied value ($/lb)[c]
CO_2	1,368	118	0.0075
NO_2	2.641	0.1020	1.04
SO_2	8.346	0.0006	1.28
PM_{10}	0.669	0.0075	0.76
VOCs	0.668	0.0054	1.48

[a]US EPA 2003, except Ottinger et al. 1990 for VOCs
[b]US EPA 1998
[c]CO_2 from CO2e.com (2005). Value for others based on the methods of Wang and Santini (1995) using emissions concentrations from US EPA (2003) and population estimates from the Metropolitan Council (2004)

stored carbon was released to the atmosphere as CO_2 in the same year (McPherson and Simpson 1999).

Calculating reduction in air pollutant emissions

Reductions in building energy use also result in reduced emission of air pollutants from power plants and space-heating equipment. Volatile organic hydrocarbons (VOCs) and nitrogen dioxide (NO_2)—both precursors of ozone formation—as well as sulfur dioxide (SO_2) and particulate matter of <10 micron diameter (PM_{10}) were considered. Changes in average annual emissions and their monetary values were calculated in the same way as for CO_2, using utility-specific emissions factors for electricity and heating fuels (Ottinger et al. 1990; US EPA 1998). The price of emissions savings were derived from models that calculate the marginal cost of controlling different pollutants to meet air quality standards (Wang and Santini 1995). Emissions concentrations were obtained from US EPA (2003; *Table C1*), and population estimates from the US Census Bureau (2005).

Calculating pollutant uptake by trees

Trees also remove pollutants from the atmosphere. The modeling method we applied was developed by Scott et al. (1998). It calculates **hourly pollutant dry deposition** per tree expressed as the product of deposition velocity ($Vd = 1/[Ra + Rb + Rc]$), pollutant concentration (C), canopy-projection area (CP), and a time step, where Ra, Rb and Rc are aerodynamic, boundary layer, and stomatal resistances. Hourly deposition velocities for each pollutant were calculated during the growing season using estimates for the resistances ($Ra + Rb + Rc$) for each hour throughout the year. Hourly concentrations for NO_2, SO_2, O_3 and PM_{10} and hourly meteorological data (i.e., air temperature, wind speed, solar radiation) from Charleston and the surrounding area for 2003 were obtained from the South Carolina Department of Environmental Quality. The year 2003 was chosen because data were available and it closely approximated long-term, regional climate records. To set a value for pollutant uptake by trees we used the procedure described above for emissions reductions (*Table C1*). The monetary value for NO_2 was used for ozone.

Estimating BVOC emissions from trees

Annual emissions for biogenic volatile organic compounds (BVOCs) were estimated for the three tree species using the algorithms of Guenther et al. (1991, 1993). Annual emissions were simulated during the growing season over 40 years. The emission of carbon as isoprene was expressed as a product of the base emission rate (μg C/g dry foliar biomass/hr), adjusted for sunlight and temperature and the amount of dry, foliar biomass present in the tree. Monoterpene emissions were estimated using a base emission rate adjusted for temperature. The base emission rates for the three species were based on values reported in the literature (Benjamin and Winer 1998). Hourly emissions were summed to get monthly and annual emissions.

Annual dry foliar biomass was derived from field data collected in Charleston, SC, during the summer of 2004 . The amount of foliar biomass present for each year of the simulated tree's life was unique for each species. Hourly air temperature and solar radiation data for 2003 described in the pollutant uptake section were used as model inputs.

Calculating net air-quality benefits

Net air-quality benefits were calculated by subtracting the costs associated with BVOC emissions from benefits due to pollutant uptake and avoided power plant emissions. The ozone-reduction benefit from lowering summertime air temperatures, thereby reducing hydrocarbon emissions from **anthropogenic** and biogenic sources were estimated as a function of canopy cover following McPherson and Simpson (1999). They used peak summer air temperatures reductions of 0.4°F for each percentage increase in canopy cover. Hourly changes in air temperature were calculated by reducing this peak air temperature at every hour based on hourly maximum and minimum temperature for that day, the maximum and minimum values of total global solar radiation for the year. Simulation results from Los Angeles indicate that ozone reduction benefits of tree planting with "low-emitting" species exceeded costs associated with their BVOC emissions (Taha 1996).

Stormwater Benefits

Estimating rainfall interception by tree canopies

A numerical simulation model was used to estimate annual rainfall interception (Xiao et al. 2000). The interception model accounted for water intercepted by the tree, as well as throughfall and **stem flow**. Intercepted water is stored temporarily on canopy leaf and bark surfaces. Rainwater drips from leaf surfaces and flows down the stem surface to the ground or evaporates. Tree-canopy parameters that affect interception include species, leaf and stem surface areas, **shade coefficients** (visual density of the crown), foliation periods, and tree dimensions (e.g., tree height, crown height, crown diameter, and DBH). Tree-height data were used to estimate wind speed at different heights above the ground and resulting rates of evaporation.

The volume of water stored in the tree crown was calculated from crown-projection area (area under tree dripline), **leaf area indices** (LAI, the ratio of leaf surface area to crown projection area), and the depth of water captured by the canopy surface. Gap fractions, foliation periods, and tree surface saturation storage capacity influence the amount of projected throughfall. Tree surface saturation was 0.04 inches (0.10 cm) for all trees. Hourly meteorological and rainfall data for 2003 at the Youmans Farm climate monitoring station (SCAN, site number: 2038, latitude: 32° 40' N, longitude: 81° 12' W, elevation: 75 feet) in Hampton County, SC, were used in this simulation. The year 2003 was chosen because it most closely approximated the 30-yr average rainfall of 52 in (1,320 mm). Annual precipitation at Youman's Farm during 2003, however, was 61.2 in (1,554.7 mm); we made use of this dataset because it was the most complete available. Storm events less than 0.2 in (5.1 mm) were assumed not to produce runoff and were dropped from the analysis. More complete descriptions of the interception model can be found in Xiao et al. (1998, 2000).

Calculating water quality protection and flood control benefit

The benefits that result from reduced peak runoff include reduced property damage from flooding and reduced loss of soil and habitat due to erosion and sediment flow. Reduced runoff also results in improved water quality in streams, lakes, and rivers. This can translate into improved aquatic habitats, less human illness due to contact with contaminated water and reduced stormwater treatment costs.

Charleston, SC, assesses monthly stormwater fees to cover the costs of its stormwater management program. These fees are used as a proxy for the public's willingness to pay for stormwater management. Residential and commercial customers are charged monthly $4 per 2,200 ft^2 of impervious surface, which is $79.20 per acre of impervious surface (McCrary 2005). The cost of controlling runoff from a 10-year storm is used as the basis for valuing rainfall interception by trees in Charleston. This event is selected because most Best Management Practices (BMPs), such as retention-detention basins, are designed to operate effectively for storm events up to this size. Runoff from larger events are assumed to bypass BMPs, directly entering the system without pretreatment. Also, tree crown interception does not increase after crowns are saturated, which usually occurs well before storm events reach this magnitude.

Runoff from 1 acre of impervious surface for a 10-year, 24-hour storm event (6.8 inches, South Carolina Department of Health and Environmental Control 2003) is 156,975 gals (594 m^3), assuming an average runoff coefficient of 0.85. Assuming an annual stormwater management fee of $950.40 per acre of impervious surface, the resulting control cost is $0.00605 per gal ($1.60 per m^3).

Aesthetic and Other Benefits

Many benefits attributed to urban trees are difficult to translate into economic terms. Beautification, privacy, wildlife habitat, shade that increases human comfort, sense of place and well-being are services that are difficult to price. However, the value of some of these benefits may be captured in the property values of the land on which trees stand.

To estimate the value of these "other" benefits, we applied results of research that compared differences in sales prices of houses to statistically quantify the difference associated with trees. All else being equal, the difference in sales price reflects the willingness of buyers to pay for the benefits and costs associated with trees. This approach has the virtue of capturing in the sales price both the benefits and costs of trees as perceived by the buyers. Limitations to this approach include difficulty determining the value of individual trees on a property, the need to extrapolate results from studies done years ago, and the need to extrapolate results from front-yard trees on residential properties to trees in other locations (e.g., back yards, streets, parks, and non-residential land).

A large tree adds value to a home

Anderson and Cordell (1988) surveyed 844 single-family residences in Athens, Georgia, and found that each large front-yard tree was associated with a 0.88% increase in the average home sales price. This percentage of sales price was utilized as an indicator of the additional value a resident in the Coastal Plain region would gain from selling a home with a large tree.

The median sales price of residential properties did not vary widely by location within the region; for example, in 2004 median home prices ranged from $110,000 in Shreveport, LA, to $320,000 in Hilton Head, SC (National Association of Realtors 2005) By averaging the values for seven cities we calculated the average median home price for Coastal Plain communities as $158,000. Therefore, the value of a large tree that added 0.88% to the sales price of such a home was $1,393. In order to estimate annual benefits, the total added value was divided by the leaf surface area of a 25-year-old live oak ($1,393/2,758 ft^2) to yield the base value of LSA, $0.51/ft^2 ($5.49 m^2). This value was multiplied by the amount of leaf surface area added to the tree during one year of growth.

Calculating the aesthetic and other benefits of residential yard trees

To calculate the base value for a large tree on private residential property we assumed that a 25-year-old live oak in the front yard increased the property sales price by $1,393. Approximately 75% of all yard trees, however, are in backyards (Richards et al. 1984). Lacking specific research findings, it was assumed that backyard trees had 75% of the impact on "curb appeal" and sales price compared to front-yard trees. The average annual aesthetic and other benefits for a tree on private property were estimated as $0.38/ft^2 ($4.11/m^2) LSA. To estimate annual benefits, this value was multiplied by the amount of leaf surface area added to the tree during one year of growth.

Calculating the aesthetic value of a public tree

The base value of street trees was calculated in the same way as yard trees. However, because street trees may be adjacent to land with little resale potential, an adjusted value was calculated. An analysis of street trees in Modesto, CA, sampled from aerial photographs (sample size 8%), found that 15% were located adjacent to nonresidential or commercial property (McPherson et al. 1999b). We assumed that 33% of these trees—or 5% of the entire street-tree population—produced no benefits associated with property value increases.

Additionally, not all street trees are as effective as front-yard trees in increasing property values. For example, trees adjacent to multifamily housing units will not increase the property value at the same rate as trees in front of single-family homes. Therefore, a citywide street tree reduction factor (0.93) was applied to prorate trees' value based on the assumption that trees adjacent to different land-uses make different contributions to property sales prices. For this analysis, the street reduction factor reflects the distribution of street trees in Charleston by land-use. Reduction factors were single-home residential (100%), multi-home residential (70%), small commercial (66%), industrial/instititutional/large commercial (40%), park/vacant/other (40%) (Gonzales 2004, McPherson 2001).

Although the impact of parks on real estate values has been reported (Hammer et al. 1974; Schroeder 1982; Tyrvainen 1999), to our knowledge the on-site and external benefits of park trees alone have not been isolated (More et al. 1988). After reviewing the literature and recognizing an absence of data, we made the conservative estimate that park trees had half the impact on property prices of street trees.

Given these assumptions, typical large street and park trees were estimated to increase property values by $0.47 and $0.25/ft^2 ($5.06 and $2.72/m^2) LSA, respectively. Assuming that 80% of all municipal trees were on streets and 20% in parks, a weighted average benefit of $0.426/ft^2 ($4.59/m^2) LSA was calculated for each tree.

Calculating Costs

Tree management costs were estimated based on surveys with municipal foresters from Jacksonville, FL; Savannah, GA; and Charleston,

SC. In addition, commercial arborists in Houston, TX; Summerville, SC; and coastal GA provided information on tree management costs on residential properties

Planting

Planting costs include the cost of the tree and the cost for planting, staking, and mulching the tree. Based on our survey of Coastal Plain municipal and commercial arborists, planting costs depend on tree size. Costs ranged from $150 for a 15-gallon tree to $550 for a 4-in tree. In this analysis we assumed that a 15-gallon yard tree was planted at a cost of $200. The cost for planting a 2.5-in (6-cm) public tree was $150.

Pruning

Pruning costs for public trees

After studying data from municipal forestry programs and their contractors, we assumed that young public trees were inspected and pruned 1.25 times during the first 5 years after planting, at a cost of $20 per tree. After this training period, pruning occurred once every 7 years for small trees (< 20 ft tall) at a cost of $25 per tree. Medium trees (20–40 ft tall) were inspected/pruned every 10 years, and large trees (> 40 ft tall) every 10 years. More expensive equipment and more time was required to prune medium ($75 per tree) and large trees ($275 per tree) than small trees. Conifers require much less substantial pruning, usually only raising of lower branches which can be accomplished from the ground. The price was set, therefore, equal to that of training ($20 per tree). After factoring in pruning frequency, annualized costs were $5, $3.75, $7.50, and $27.50 per tree for public young, small, medium, and large broadleaf trees, respectively and $5 per tree for conifers.

Pruning costs for yard trees

Based on findings from our survey of commercial arborists in the Coastal Plain region, pruning cycles for yard trees were slightly more frequent than public trees, but only about 20% of all private trees were professionally pruned (**contract rate**). However, the number of professionally pruned trees grows as the trees grow. We assumed that professionals are paid to prune all large trees, 60% of the medium trees, and only 6% of the small and young trees and conifers (Summit and McPherson 1998). Using these contract rates, along with average pruning prices ($45, $75, $225, and $500 for young, small, medium, and large trees, respectively), the average annual costs for pruning a yard tree were $0.21, $0.32, $6.21, and $21.00 for young, small, medium, and large trees. Pruning of private conifers was calculated as above for public trees and valued as $0.21 per tree per year.

Tree and Stump Removal

The costs for tree removal and disposal were $20 per inch ($7.87 per cm) DBH for public trees, and $35 per inch ($13.78 per cm) DBH for yard trees. Stump removal costs were $5 per inch ($1.96 per cm) DBH for public and yard trees. Therefore, total costs for removal and disposal of trees and stumps were $25 per inch ($9.84 per cm) DBH for public trees, and $40 per inch ($15.75 per cm) DBH for yard trees. Removal costs of trees under 3 inches (7.5 cm) in diameter were $30 and $40 for yard and public trees, respectively.

Pest and Disease Control

Pest and disease control measures in the Coastal Plain are minimal. No city surveyed included costs for pest and disease control in its budget. Results of our commercial arborists' survey indicated that only 1% of all yard trees were treated, and the amount of money spent averaged $45 per tree. The estimated cost for treating pests and diseases in yard trees was $0.45 per tree per year or $.0495 per inch ($0.0194 per cm) DBH.

Irrigation Costs

Rain falls fairly regularly (4–5 in/month) throughout most of the Coastal Plain region and in sufficient quantities that irrigation is not usually needed. None of the municipalities surveyed provided irrigation to street trees beyond the first two years. The average watering costs for the first two years was $12.50 per tree or about $0.61 per tree annualized over 40 years.

Other Costs for Public and Yard Trees

Other costs associated with the management of trees include expenditures for infrastructure repair/root pruning, leaf-litter clean-up, and inspection/administration.

Infrastructure conflict costs

Many Coastal Plain municipalities have a substantial number of large, old trees and deteriorating sidewalks. As trees and sidewalks age, roots can cause damage to sidewalks, curbs, paving, and sewer lines. Sidewalk repair is typically one of the largest expenses for public trees (McPherson and Peper 1995). Infrastructure-related expenditures for public trees in Coastal Plain communities were approximately $1.50 per tree on an annual basis. Roots from most trees in yards do not damage sidewalks and sewers. Therefore, the cost for yard trees was estimated to be only 10% of the cost for public trees.

Litter and storm clean-up costs

The average annual per tree cost for litter clean-up (i.e., street sweeping, storm-damage clean-up) was $0.70 per tree ($0.077/in [$0.0303 per cm] DBH). This value was based on average annual litter clean-up costs and storm clean-up, assuming a large storm results in extraordinary costs about once a decade. Because most residential yard trees are not littering the streets with leaves, it was assumed that clean-up costs for yard trees were 10% of those for public trees.

Inspection and administration costs

Municipal tree programs have administrative costs for salaries of supervisors and clerical staff, operating costs, and overhead. Our survey found that the average annual cost for inspection and administration associated with street- and park-tree management was $2 per tree ($0.22/in [$0.086/cm] DBH). Trees on private property do not accrue this expense.

Calculating Net Benefits

Benefits Accrue at Different Scales

When calculating net benefits, it is important to recognize that trees produce benefits that accrue both on- and off-site. Benefits are realized at four different scales: parcel, neighborhood, community, and global. For example, property owners with on-site trees not only benefit from increased property values, but they may also directly benefit from improved human health (e.g., reduced exposure to cancer-causing UV radiation) and greater psychological well-being through visual and direct contact with plants. However, on the cost side, increased health care may be incurred because of nearby trees due to allergies and respiratory ailments related to pollen. We assume that these intangible benefits and costs are reflected in what we term "aesthetics and other benefits."

The property owner can obtain additional economic benefits from on-site trees depending on their location and condition. For example, carefully located on-site trees can provide air-conditioning savings by shading windows and walls and cooling building microclimates. This benefit can extend to adjacent neighbors who benefit from shade and air-temperature reductions that lower their cooling costs.

Neighborhood attractiveness and property values can be influenced by the extent of tree canopy cover on individual properties. At the community scale, benefits are realized through cleaner air and water, as well as social, educational, and employment and job training benefits that can reduce costs for health care, welfare, crime prevention, and other social service programs.

Reductions in atmospheric CO_2 concentrations due to trees are an example of benefits that are realized at the global scale.

Annual benefits are calculated as:

The sum of all benefits is…

$$B = E + AQ + CO_2 + H + A \quad \text{where}$$

E = value of net annual energy savings (cooling and heating)

AQ = value of annual air-quality improvement (pollutant uptake, avoided power plant emissions, and BVOC emissions)

CO_2 = value of annual carbon dioxide reductions (sequestration, avoided emissions, release due to tree care and decomposition)

H = value of annual stormwater-runoff reductions

A = value of annual aesthetics and other benefits

On the other side of the benefit–cost equation are costs for tree planting and management. Expenditures are borne by property owners (irrigation, pruning, and removal) and the community (pollen and other health care costs). Annual costs (C) are the sum of costs for residential yard trees (C_Y) and public trees (C_P) where:

The sum of all costs is…

$$C_Y = P + T + R + D + I + S + Cl + L$$
$$C_P = P + T + R + D + I + S + Cl + L + A \quad \text{where}$$

P = cost of tree and planting

T = average annual tree pruning cost

R = annualized tree and stump removal and disposal cost

D = average annual pest- and disease-control cost

I = annual irrigation cost

S = average annual cost to repair/mitigate infrastructure damage

Cl = annual litter and storm clean-up cost

L = average annual cost for litigation and settlements due to tree-related claims

A = annual program administration, inspection, and other costs

Net benefits are calculated as the difference between total benefits and costs:

Net benefits are…

Net benefits = $B – C$

Benefit–cost ratios (BCR) are calculated as the ratio of benefits to costs:

$$BCR = B / C$$

Limitations of This Study

This analysis does not account for the wide variety of trees planted in Coastal Plain communities or their diverse placement. It does not incorporate the full range of climatic differences within the region that influence potential energy, air-quality, and hydrology benefits. Estimating aesthetics and other benefits is difficult because the science in this area is not well developed. We considered only residential and municipal tree cost scenarios, but realize that the costs associated with planting and managing trees can vary widely depending on program characteristics. For example, our analysis does not incorporate costs incurred by utility companies and passed on to customers for maintenance of trees under power lines. However, as described by examples in Chapter 3, local cost data can be substituted for the data in this report to evaluate the benefits and costs of alternative programs.

More research is needed

In this analysis, results are presented in terms of future values of benefits and costs, not present values. Thus, findings do not incorporate the time value of money or inflation. We assume that the user intends to invest in community forests and our objective is to identify the relative magnitudes of future costs and benefits. If the user is interested in comparing an investment in urban forestry with other investment opportunities, it is important to discount all future benefits and costs to the beginning of the investment period. For example, trees with a future value of $100,000 in 10 years have a present value of $55,840, assuming a 6% annual interest rate.

Future benefits are not discounted to present value

Glossary of Terms

Annual fuel utilization efficiency (AFUE): A measure of space heating equipment efficiency defined as the fraction of energy output/energy input.

Anthropogenic: Produced by humans.

Avoided power plant emissions: Reduced emissions of CO_2 or other pollutants that result from reductions in building energy use due to the moderating effect of trees on climate. Reduced energy use for heating and cooling results in reduced demand for electrical energy, which translates into fewer emissions by power plants.

Biodiversity: The variety of life forms in a given area. Diversity can be categorized in terms of the number of species, the variety in the area's plant and animal communities, the genetic variability of the animals or plants, or a combination of these elements.

Biogenic: Produced by living organisms.

Biogenic volatile organic compounds (BVOCs): Hydrocarbon compounds from vegetation (e.g., isoprene, monoterpene) that exist in the ambient air and contribute to the formation of smog and/or may themselves be toxic. Emission rates (ug/g/hr) used for this report follow Benjamin and Winer (1998):

Acer rubrum: 0.0 (isoprene); 2.8 (monoterpene)
Magnolia grandiflora: 0.0 (isoprene); 5.9 (monoterpene)
Cornus florida: 0.0 (isoprene); 0.0 (monoterpene)
Pinus taeda: 0.0 (isoprene); 5.1 (monoterpene)

Canopy: A layer or multiple layers of branches and foliage at the top or crown of a forest's trees.

Canopy cover: The area of land surface that is covered by tree canopy, as seen from above.

Climate: The average weather for a particular region and time period (usually 30 years). Weather describes the short-term state of the atmosphere; climate is the average pattern of weather for a particular region. Climatic elements include precipitation, temperature, humidity, sunshine, wind velocity, phenomena such as fog, frost, and hail storms, and other measures of weather.

Climate effects: Impact on residential energy use (kg CO_2 per tree per year) from trees located more than 50 ft (15 m) from a building due to reductions in wind speeds and summer air temperatures.

Community forests: The sum of all woody and associated vegetation in and around human settlements, ranging from small rural villages to metropolitan regions.

Conifer: A tree that bears cones and has needle-like leaves.

Contract rate: The percentage of residential trees cared for by commercial arborists; the proportion of trees contracted out for a specific service (e.g., pruning or pest management).

Control costs: The marginal cost of reducing air pollutants or controlling stormwater using best available control technologies.

Crown: The branches and foliage at the top of a tree.

Cultivar: Derived from "cultivated variety." Denotes certain cultivated plants that are clearly distinguishable from others by any characteristic, and that when reproduced (sexually or asexually), retain their distinguishing characteristics. In the United States, variety is often considered synonymous with cultivar.

Damage costs: The marginal costs of damage directly related to exposure to increased pollutants.

Deciduous: Trees or shrubs that lose their leaves every fall.

Diameter at breast height (DBH): The diameter of a tree outside the bark measured 4.5 feet (1.37 m) above the ground on the uphill side (where applicable) of the tree.

Emission factor: The rate of CO_2, NO_2, SO_2, and PM_{10} output resulting from the consumption of electricity, natural gas or any other fuel source.

Evapotranspiration (ET): The total loss of water by evaporation from the soil surface and by transpiration from plants, from a given area, and during a specified period of time.

Evergreens: Trees or shrubs that are never entirely leafless. Evergreens may be broadleaved or coniferous (cone-bearing with needle-like leaves).

Greenspace: Urban trees, forests, and associated vegetation in and around human settlements, ranging from small communities in rural settings to metropolitan regions.

Hardscape: Paving and other impervious ground surfaces that reduce infiltration of water in to the soil.

Heat sink: Paving, buildings, and other built surfaces that store heat energy from the sun.

Hourly pollutant dry deposition: Removal of gases from the atmosphere by direct transfer to natural surfaces and absorption of gases and particles by natural surfaces such as vegetation, soil, water or snow.

Interception: Amount of rainfall held on tree leaves and stem surfaces.

kBtu: A unit of heat, measured as 1,000 British thermal units. One kBtu is equivalent to 0.293 kWh.

kWh (kilowatt-hour): A unit of work or energy, measured as one kilowatt (1,000 watts) of power expended for one hour. One kWh is equivalent to 3.412 kBtu.

Leaf surface area (LSA): Measurement of area of one side of a leaf or leaves.

Mature tree: A tree that has reached a desired size or age for its intended use. Size, age, or economic maturity varies depending on the species, location, growing conditions, and intended use.

Mature tree size: Approximate size of a tree 40 years after planting.

MBtu: A unit of work or energy, measured as 1,000,000 British thermal units. One MBtu is equivalent to 0.293 MWh.

Metric tonne (t): A measure of weight equal to 1,000,000 grams (1,000 kilograms) or 2,205 pounds.

Municipal forester: A person who manages public street and/or park trees (municipal forestry programs) for the benefit of the community.

MWh (megawatt-hour): A unit of work or energy, measured as one Megawatt (1,000,000 watts) of power expended for one hour. One MWh is equivalent to 3.412 Mbtu.

Nitrogen oxides (oxides of nitrogen, NOx): A general term for compounds of nitric acid (NO), nitrogen dioxide (NO_2), and other oxides of nitrogen. Nitrogen oxides are typically created during combustion processes and are major contributors to smog formation and acid deposition. NO_2 may cause numerous adverse human health effects.

Ozone: A strong-smelling, pale blue, reactive toxic chemical gas consisting of three oxygen atoms. It is a product of the photochemical process involving the sun's energy. Ozone exists in the upper layer of the atmosphere as well as at the earth's surface. Ozone at the earth's surface can cause numerous adverse human health effects. It is a major component of smog.

Peak cooling demand: The greatest amount of electricity required at any one time during the course of a year to meet space cooling requirements.

Peak flow (or peak runoff): The maximum rate of runoff at a given point or from a given area, during a specific period.

Photosynthesis: The process in green plants of converting water and carbon dioxide into sugar with light energy; accompanied by the production of oxygen.

PM_{10} (particulate matter): Major class of air pollutants consisting of tiny solid or liquid particles of soot, dust, smoke, fumes, and mists. The size of the particles (10 microns or smaller, about 0.0004 inches or less) allows them to enter the air sacs (gas-exchange region) deep in the lungs where they may be deposited and cause adverse health effects. PM_{10} also reduces visibility.

Resource unit (RU): The value used to determine and calculate benefits and costs of individual trees. For example, the amount of air conditioning energy saved in kWh/yr per tree, air-pollutant uptake in pounds per tree per year, or rainfall intercepted in gallons per tree per year.

Riparian habitat: Narrow strips of land bordering creeks, rivers, lakes, or other bodies of water.

SEER (seasonal energy efficiency ratio): Ratio of cooling output to power consumption; kBtu-output/kWh-input as a fraction. It is the Btu of cooling output during normal annual usage divided by the total electric energy input in kilowatt-hours during the same period.

Sequestration: Annual net rate that a tree removes CO_2 from the atmosphere through the processes of photosynthesis and respiration (kg CO_2 per tree per year).

Shade coefficient: The percentage of light striking a tree crown that is transmitted through gaps in the crown. This is the percentage of light that hits the ground.

Shade effects: Impact on residential space heating and cooling (kg CO_2 per tree per year) from trees located within 50 ft (50 m) of a building.

Solar-friendly trees: Trees that have characteristics that reduce blocking of winter sunlight. According to one numerical ranking system, these traits include open crowns during the winter heating season, leaves that fall early and appear late, relatively small size, and a slow growth rate (Ames 1987).

Sulfur dioxide (SO_2): A strong-smelling, colorless gas that is formed by the combustion of fossil fuels. Power plants, which may use coal or oil high in sulfur content, can be major sources of SO_2. Sulfur oxides contribute to the problem of acid deposition.

Stem flow: Amount of rainfall that travels down the tree trunk and onto the ground.

Therm: A unit of heat equal to 100,000 British thermal units (BTUs) or 100 kBtu. Also, 1 kBtu is equal to 0.01 therm.

Throughfall: Amount of rainfall that falls directly to the ground below the tree crown or drips onto the ground from branches and leaves.

Transpiration: The loss of water vapor through leaf stomata.

Tree or canopy cover: Within a specific area, the percentage covered by the crown of an individual tree or delimited by the vertical projection of its outermost perimeter; small openings in the crown are ignored. Used to express the relative importance of individual species within a vegetation community or to express the coverage of woody species.

Tree litter: Fruit, leaves, twigs, and other debris shed by trees.

Tree-related emissions: Carbon dioxide released when growing, planting, and caring for trees.

Tree height: Total height of tree from base (at groundline) to treetop.

Tree-surface saturation storage (or tree-surface detention): The maximum volume of water that can be stored on a tree's leaves, stems and bark. This part of rainfall stored on the canopy surface does not contribute to surface runoff during and after a rainfall event.

Urban heat island: An area in a city where summertime air temperatures are 3 to 8°F warmer than temperatures in the surrounding countryside. Urban areas are warmer for two reasons: (1) Dark construction materials for roofs and asphalt absorb solar energy, and (2) there are few trees, shrubs or other vegetation to provide shade and cool the air.

VOCs (volatile organic compounds): Hydrocarbon compounds that exist in the ambient air. VOCs contribute to the formation of smog and/or are toxic. VOCs often have an odor. Some examples of VOCs are gasoline, alcohol, and the solvents used in paints.

Willingness to pay: The maximum amount of money an individual would be willing to pay, rather than do without, for non-market, public goods and services provided by environmental amenities such as trees and forests.

References

Akbari, H.; Davis, S.; Dorsano, S.; Huang, J.; Winnett, S. (Eds.). 1992. Cooling Our Communities: A Guidebook on Tree Planting and Light-Colored Surfacing. Washington, DC: U.S. Environmental Protection Agency. 26 pp.

American Forests. 2002. Urban Ecological Analysis, New Orleans, LA Metropolitan Area. Washington, DC: American Forests. 4 pp.

American Forests. 2004. Urban Ecological Analysis, Montgomery, AL. Washington, DC: American Forests. 12 pp.

American Forests. 2005. Urban Ecosystem Analysis, Jacksonville, FL. Washington, DC: American Forests. 12 pp.

Ames, M.J. 1987. Solar Friendly Trees Report. Portland, OR: City of Portland Energy Office.

Anderson, L.M.; Cordell, H.K. 1988. Residential property values improve by landscaping with trees. Southern Journal of Applied Forestry. 9:162–166.

Benjamin, M.T.; Winer, A.M. 1998. Estimating the ozone-forming potential of urban trees and shrubs. Atmos. Environ. 32:53–68.

Bernhardt, E.; Swiecki, T.J. 1993. The State of Urban Forestry in California: Results of the 1992 California Urban Forest Survey. Sacramento: California Department of Forestry and Fire Protection. 51 pp.

Brenzel, K.N. (Ed.). 2001. Sunset Western Garden Book. 7th ed. Menlo Park, CA: Sunset Books Inc.

Burbage, D. 2005. Personal communication. Urban Forestry Superintendent, City of Charleston, SC.

Cappiella, K.; Schueler, T.; Wright, T. 2005. Urban Watershed Forestry Manual. Ellicot City, MD: Center for Watershed Protection.

Cardelino, C.A., Chameides, W.L. 1990. Natural hydrocarbons, urbanization, and urban ozone. Journal of Geophysical Research. 95(9):13971–13979.

Chameides, W.L.; Lindsay, R.W.; Richardson, J.; Kiang, C.S. 1988. The role of biogenic hydrocarbons in urban photochemical smog: Atlanta as a case study. Science. 241: 1473–1475.

CO2e.com. 2005. CO2e Market Size and Pricing. Accessed via the World Wide Web <http://www.co2e.com/strategies/AdditionalInfo.asp?PageID=273#1613> on September 8, 2005.

Cohen, J.E.; Small, C.; Mellinger, A.; Gallup, J.; Sachs, J. 1997. Estimates of coastal populations. Science. 278(5341):1211–1212

Cook, D.I. 1978. Trees, solid barriers, and combinations: Alternatives for noise control. In: Proceedings of the National Urban Forestry Conference. ESF Pub. 80-003. Syracuse, NY: SUNY: 330–334.

Costello, L.R. 2000. Training Young Trees for Structure and Form. Videotape Number: V99-A. University of California, Agriculture and Natural Resources, Communication Services Cooperative Extension Service, Oakland, CA. (Telephone: 800-994-8849).

Costello, L.R.; Jones, K.S. 2003. Reducing Infrastructure Damage by Tree Roots: A Compendium of Strategies. Cohasset, CA: Western Chapter of the International Society of Arboriculture.

Duryea, M.L. 1997. Wind and trees: surveys of tree damage in the Florida Panhandle after Hurricanes Erin and Opal. Circular 1183. Gainesville, FL: Florida Cooperative Extension Service. University of Florida, Gainesville.

Dwyer, M.C.; Miller, R.W. 1999. Using GIS to assess urban tree canopy benefits and surrounding greenspace distributions. J. Arboric. 25(2):102–107.

Dwyer, J.F.; McPherson, E.G.; Schroeder, H.W.; Rowntree, R.A. 1992. Assessing the benefits and costs of the urban forest. J. Arboric. 18(5):227–234.

Gilman, E.F. 1997. Trees for Urban and Suburban Landscapes. Albany, NY: Delmar.

Gilman, E.F. 2002. An Illustrated Guide to Pruning. 2nd ed. Albany, NY: Delmar. Gonzalez, S. 2004. Personal communication on September 23, 2004 re Landscape Assessment Districts method of apportionment. Landscape Maintenance Manager, Vallejo, CA.

Gonzalez, S. 2004. Personal communication. Landscape Maintenance Manager, Vallejo, CA.

Guenther, A.B.; Monson, R.K.; Fall, R. 1991. Isoprene and monoterpene emission rate variability: observations with eucalyptus and emission rate algorithm development. Journal of Geophysical Research. 96: 10799–10808.

Guenther, A.B.; Zimmermann, P.R.; Harley, P.C.; Monson, R.K.; Fall, R. 1993. Isoprene and monoterpene emission rate variability: model evaluations and sensitivity analyses. Journal of Geophysical Research. 98:12609–12617.

Hamburg, S.P.; Harris, N.; Jaeger, J.; Karl, T.R.; McFarland, M.; Mitchell, J.; Oppenheimer, M.; Santer, B.; Schneider, S.; Trenberth, K.; Wigley, T. 1997. Common Questions About Climate Change. Nairobi, Kenya: United Nations Envirnment Programme, World Meteorological Organization. 22 pp.

Hammer, T.T.; Coughlin, R.; Horn, E. 1974. The effect of a large urban park on real estate value. Journal of the American Institute of Planning. July:274–275.

Hammond J.; Zanetto, J.; Adams, C. 1980. Planning Solar Neighborhoods. California Energy Commission.

Harris, R.W.; Clark, J.R.; Matheny, N.P. 1999. Arboriculture. 3rd ed. Englewood Cliffs, NJ: Regents/Prentice Hall.

Heisler, G.M. 1986. Energy savings with trees. J. Arboric. 12(5):113–125.

Hightshoe, G.L. 1988. Native Trees, Shrubs, and Vines for Urban and Rural America. New York: Van Nostrand Reinhold.

Hildebrandt, E.W.; Kallett, R.; Sarkovich, M.; Sequest, R. 1996. Maximizing the energy benefits of urban forestation. In: Proceedings of the ACEEE 1996 summer study on energy efficiency in buildings, volume 9; Washington DC: American Council for an Energy Efficient Economy: 121–131.

Hudson, B. 1983. Private sector business analogies applied in urban forestry. J. Arboric. 9(10):253–258.

Hull, R.B. 1992. How the public values urban forests. J. Arboric. 18(2):98–101.

IPCC (Intergovernmental Panel on Climate Change). 2001. Technical Summary. Climate Change 2001: The Scientific Basis. IPCC, Geneva. Accessed via the World Wide Web <http://www.ipcc.ch/pub/reports.htm> on December 19, 2005.

ISA. 1992. Avoiding tree and utility conflicts. Savoy, IL: International Society of Arboriculture. 4 pp.

Jo, H.K.; McPherson, E.G. 1995. Carbon storage and flux in residential greenspace. J. Environ. Manage. 45:109–133.

Kaplan, R. 1992. Urban Forestry and the Workplace. In: Gobster, P.H. (Ed.). Managing Urban and High-Use Recreation Settings. USDA Forest Service, General Technical Report NC-163. Chicago, IL: North Central Forest Experiment Station.

Kaplan, R.; Kaplan, S. 1989. The Experience of Nature: A Psychological Perspective. Cambridge, UK: Cambridge University Press.

Kim, S.; Byun, D.W.; Cheng, F.-Y.; Czader, B.; Stetson, S.; Nowak, D.; Walton, J.; Estes, M.; Hitchcock, D. 2005. Modeling Effects of Land Use Land Cover Changes on Meteorology and Air Quality in Houston, Texas, Over the Two Decades. Proc. 2005 Atmos Sci Air Qual Conf, San Francisco. Available at <http://ams.confex.com/ams/pdfpapers/92244.pdf.

Lewis, C.A. 1996. Green Nature/Human Nature: The Meaning of Plants in Our Lives. Chicago, IL: University of Illinois Press.

Luley, C.J.; Bond, J. 2002. A Plan to Integrate Management of Urban Trees into Air Quality Planning. Naples, NY: Davey Resource Group. 61 pp.

Maco, S.E.; McPherson, E.G. 2003. A practical approach to assessing structure, function, and value of street tree populations in small communities. J. Arboric. 29(2):84–97.

Marion, W.; Urban, K. 1995. User's Manual for TMY2s—Typical Meteorological Years. Golden, CO: National Renewable Energy Laboratory.

Markwardt, L.J. 1930. Comparative Strength Properties of Woods Grown in the United States. Tech. Bull. No. 158. Washington, DC: U.S. Department of Agriculture.

McCrary, S. 2005. Personal communication. Project Manager, City of Charleston, Dept. of Public Service, April 21, 2005.

McHale, M. 2003. Carbon credit markets: Is there a role for community forestry? In: Kollin, C. ed. 2003 National Urban Forest Conference Proceedings. Washington, DC: American Forests: 74–77.

McNab, W.H., Avers, P.E. 1994. Ecological Subregions of the United States. WO-WSA-5. Washington, DC: U.S. Department of Agriculture, Forest Service.

McPherson, E.G. 1984. Planting design for solar control. Chapter 8. In: Energy Conserving Site Design. Washington, DC: Am. Soc. Landscape Archit: 141-164.

McPherson, E.G. 1992. Accounting for benefits and costs of urban greenspace. Landscape and Urban Planning. 22:41–51.

McPherson, E.G. 1993. Evaluating the cost effectiveness of shade trees for demand-side management. The Electricity Journal. 6(9):57–65.

McPherson, E.G. 1995. Net benefits of healthy and productive forests. In: Bradley, G.A. (Ed.). Urban Forest Landscapes: Integrating Multidisciplinary Perspectives. Seattle, WA: University of Washington Press: 180–194.

McPherson, E.G. 1997. Airing it out. Spring Update. Davis, CA: U.S. Department of Agriculture, Forest Service, Pacific Southwest Research Station, Center for Urban Forest Research. 4 pp.

McPherson, E.G. 1998. Atmospheric carbon dioxide reduction by Sacramento's urban forest. J. Arboric. 24(4):215–223.

McPherson, E.G. 2000. Expenditures associated with conflicts between street tree root growth and hardscape in California. J. Arboric. 26(6):289–297.

McPherson, E.G. 2001. Sacramento's parking lot shading ordinance: environmental and economic costs of compliance. Landscape and Urban Planning. 57:105–123.

McPherson, E.G.; Mathis, S. (Eds.) 1999. Proceedings of the Best of the West Summit. Sacramento, CA: Western Chapter, International Society of Arboriculture. 93 pp.

McPherson, E.G.; Muchnick, J. 2005. Effects of tree shade on asphalt concrete pavement performance. Journal of Arboriculture. 31(6):303–309.

McPherson, E.G.; Peper, P.J. 1995. Infrastructure repair costs associated with street trees in 15 cities. In: Watson, G.W., Neely, D. (Eds.). Trees and Building Sites. Champaign, IL: International Society of Arboriculture: 49–63.

McPherson, E.G., Simpson, J.R. 1999. Guidelines for Calculating Carbon Dioxide Reductions Through Urban Forestry Programs. General Technical Report No. 171. Albany, CA: U.S. Department of Agriculture, Forest Service, Pacific Southwest Research Station.

McPherson, E.G.; Simpson, J.R. 2003. Potential energy savings in buildings by an urban tree planting programme in California. Urban For. Urban Green. 2:73–86.

McPherson, E.G., Simpson, J.R. 2002. A comparison of municipal forest benefits and costs in Modesto and Santa Monica, CA, USA. Urban For. Urban Green. 1(2002): 61–74.

McPherson, E.G., Simpson, J.R. 2003. Potenial energy savings in buildings by an urban tree planting programme in California. Urban For. Urban Green. 2:73–86.

McPherson, E.G.; Sacamano, P.L.; Wensman, S. 1993. Modeling Benefits and Costs of Community Tree Plantings. Davis, CA: U.S. Department of Agriculture, Forest Service, Pacific Southwest Research Station. 170 pp.

McPherson, E.G.; Nowak, D.J.; Rowntree, R.A. 1994. Chicago's Urban Forest Ecosystem: Results of the Chicago Urban Forest Climate Project. Gen. Tech. Rep. NE-186. Radnor, PA: U.S. Department of Agriculture, Forest Service, Northeastern Forest Experiment Station. 201pp.

McPherson, E.G.; Nowak, D.J.; Heisler, G.; Grimmond, S.; Souch, C.; Grant, R; Rowntree, R.A. 1997. Quantifying urban forest structure, function, and value: The Chicago's Urban Forest Climate Project. Urban Ecosystems. 1:49–61.

McPherson, E.G.; Simpson, J.R.; Peper, P.J.; Xiao, Q. 1999a. Tree Guidelines for San Joaquin Valley Communities. Sacramento, CA: Local Government Commission. 63 pp.

McPherson, E.G.; Simpson, J.R.; Peper, P.J.; Xiao, Q. 1999b. Benefit-cost analysis of Modesto's municipal urban forest. J. Arboric. 25(5):235–248.

McPherson, E.G.; Simpson, J.R.; Peper, P.J.; Scott, K.; Xiao, Q. 2000. Tree Guidelines for Coastal Southern California Communities. Sacramento, CA: Local Government Commission. 97 pp.

McPherson, E.G.; Simpson, J.R.; Peper, P.J.; Maco, S.E.; Xiao, Q.; Hoefer, P.J. 2003. Northern Mountain and Prairie Community Tree Guide: Benefits, Costs, and Strategic Planting. Davis, CA: U.S. Department of Agriculture, Forest Service, Center for Urban Forest Research.

McPherson, E.G.; Simpson, J.R.; Peper, P.J.; Maco, S.E.; Xiao, Q.; Mulrean, E. 2004. Desert Southwest Community Tree Guide: Benefits, Costs, and Strategic Planting. Davis, CA: U.S. Department of Agriculture, Forest Service, Center for Urban Forest Research.

McPherson, E.G.; Simpson, J.R.; Peper, P.J.; Maco, S.E.; Gardner, S.L.; Cozad, S.K.; Xiao, Q. 2005a. Midwest Community Tree Guide: Benefits, Costs, and Strategic Planting. NA-TP-05-05. Newton Square, PA: U.S. Department of Agriculture, Forest Service, Northeastern Area State and Private Forestry.

McPherson, E.G.; Simpson, J.R.; Peper, P.J.; Gardner, S.L.; Vargas, K.E.; Ho, J.; Maco, S.; Xiao, Q. 2005b. City of Charlotte, North Carolina, Municipal Forest Resource Analysis. Internal Tech. Rep. Davis, CA: U.S. Department of Agriculture, Forest Service.

McPherson, E.G.; Simpson, J.R.; Peper, P.J.; Gardner, S.L.; Vargas, K.E.; Ho, J.; Maco, S.; Xiao, Q. 2006a. City of Charleston, South Carolina, Municipal Forest Resource Analysis. Internal Tech. Rep. Davis, CA: U.S. Department of Agriculture, Forest Service.

McPherson, E.G.; Simpson, J.R.; Peper, P.J.; Gardner, S.L.; Vargas, K.E.; Maco, S.E.; Xiao, Q. 2006b. Piedmont Community Tree Guide: Benefits, Costs, and Strategic Planting. Davis, CA: U.S. Department of Agriculture, Forest Service, Center for Urban Forest Research.

Metro. 2002. Green Streets: Innovative Solutions for Stormwater and Stream Crossings. Portland, OR: Metro.

Metropolitan Council. 2004. Twin Cities Area Population. Accessed via <http://www.metrocouncil.org/about/facts/TwinCitiesPopulationFacts.pdf> on Dec 12, 2004.

Miller, R.W. 1997. Urban Forestry: Planning and Managing Urban Greenspaces. 2nd Edition. Upper Saddle River, NJ: Prentice-Hall. 502 pp.

More, T.A.; Stevens, T; Allen, P.G. 1988. Valuation of urban parks. Landscape and Urban Planning. 15:139–52.

National Association of Realtors. 2005. Accessed via the World Wide Web <http http://www.realtor.org/Research.nsf/files/REL05Q3T.pdf/> February 2005.

Natural Resource Conservation Service (NRCS), Agroforestry Center. 2005. Working trees for treating waste. Western Arborist. 31:50-52.

Neely, D. (Ed.) 1988. Valuation of Landscape Trees, Shrubs, and Other Plants. Seventh. ed. Urbana, IL: International Society of Arboriculture. 50 pp.

Ning, Z.H.; Turner, R.E.; Doyle, T.; Abdollahi, K.K. 2003. Integrated Assessment of the Climate Change Impacts on the Gulf Coast Region. Baton Rouge, LA: Gulf Coast Climate Change Assessment Council and Louisiana State University.

Noble, R.D.; Martin, J.L.; Jensen, K.F. 1988. Air pollution effects on vegetation, including forest ecosystems. Proceedings of the Second US-USSR Symposium, Corvallis, OR, 1988. Gov. Doc. A13.42/2:2:A:7. Broomall, PA: Northeastern Forest Experiment Station.

Nowak, D.J. 1994. Air pollution removal by Chicago's urban forest. In: McPherson, E.G., Nowak, D.J., Rowntree, R.A. eds. Chicago's Urban Forest Ecosystem: Results of the Chicago Urban Forest Climate Project. GTR NE-186. Radnor, PA: U.S. Department of Agriculture, Forest Service, Northeastern Forest Experiment Station: 63–82.

Nowak, D.J. 2000. Tree species selection, design, and management to improve air quality. In: Scheu, D.L. (Ed.). 2000 ASLA Annual Meeting Proceedings. Washington DC: American Society of Landscape Architects:23–27.

Nowak, D.J.; Crane, D.E. 2002. Carbon storage and sequestration by urban trees in the USA. Environmental Pollution. 116: 381-389.

Nowak, D.J.; Civerolo, K.L.; Rao, S.T.; Sistla, G.; Luley, C.J.; Crane, D.E. 2000. A modeling study of the impact of urban trees on ozone. Atmosph. Envir. 34:1601–1613.

Ogden, J.C. 1992. The impact of Hurricane Andrew on the ecosystems of South Florida. Conservation Biology. 6:488–490.

Ottinger, R.L.; Wooley, D.R.; Robinson, N.A.; Hodas, D.R.; Babb, S.E. 1990. Environmental Costs of Electricity. New York: Pace University Center for Environmental Legal Studies, Oceana Publications.

Parsons, R.; Tassinary, L.G.; Ulrich, R.S.; Hebl, M.R.; Grossman-Alexander, M. 1998. The view from the road: implications for stress recovery and immunization. Journal of Environmental Psychology. 18(2):113–140.

Pearce, D. 2003. The social cost of carbon and its policy implications. Oxford Review of Economic Policy. 19(3):362–384.

Peper, P.J.; McPherson, E.G. 2003. Evaluation of four methods for estimating leaf area of isolated trees. Urban For. Urban Green. 2:19–29.

Pillsbury, N.H.; Reimer, J.L.; Thompson R.P. 1998. Tree Volume Equations for Fifteen Urban Species in California. Tech. Rpt. 7. San Luis Obispo, CA: Urban Forest Ecosystems Institute, California Polytechnic State University. 56 pp.

Platt, R.H.; Rowntree, R.A.; Muick, P.C. (Eds). 1994. The Ecological City. Boston, MA: University of Massachusetts. 292 pp.

Ramsay, S. 2002. Personal communication. Executive Director, Trees Forever, Marion, IA.

Richards, N.A.; Mallette, J.R.; Simpson, R.J.; Macie, E.A. 1984. Residential greenspace and vegetation in a mature city: Syracuse, New York. Urban Ecol. 8:99–125.

Sand, M. 1991. Planting for Energy Conservation in the North. Minneapolis: Department of Natural Resources: State of Minnesota. 19 pp.

Sand, M. 1993. Energy Conservation Through Community Forestry. St. Paul: University of Minnesota. 40 pp.

Sand, M. 1994. Design and species selection to reduce urban heat island and conserve energy. In: Proceedings from the Sixth National Urban Forest Conference: Growing Greener Communities. Minneapolis, Minnesota: Sept. 14-18, 1993. Washington DC: American Forests: 282.

SCANA Corporation. 2005a. Accessed via the World Wide Web at http://www.scana.com/SCEG/At+Home/Customer+Service/Rates/Residential+Electric+Rates.htm on 11 April 2005.

SCANA Corporation. 2005b. Accessed via the World Wide Web at <http://www.scana.com/SCEG/At+Home/Customer+Service/Rates/Residential+Gas+Rates.htm> on 11 April 2005.

Schroeder, T. 1982. The relationship of local park and recreation services to residential property values. Journal of Leisure Research. 14:223–234.

Schroeder, H.W.; Cannon, W.N. 1983. The esthetic contribution of trees to residential streets in Ohio towns. J. Arboric. 9:237–243.

Scott, K.I.; McPherson, E.G.; Simpson, J.R. 1998. Air pollutant uptake by Sacramento's urban forest. J. Arboric. 24(4):224–234.

Scott, K.I.; Simpson, J.R.; McPherson, E.G. 1999. Effects of tree cover on parking lot microclimate and vehicle emissions. J. Arboric. 25(3):129–142.

Simpson, J.R. 1998. Urban forest impacts on regional space conditioning energy use: Sacramento County case study. J. Arboric. 24(4):201–214.

Smith, W.H. 1990. Air pollution and forests. New York: Springer-Verlag. 618pp.

Smith, W.H.; Dochinger, L.S. 1976. Capability of metropolitan trees to reduce atmospheric contaminants. In: Santamour, F.S., Gerhold, H.D., Little, S. (Eds.) Better Trees for Metropolitan Landscapes. GTR NE-22. Upper Darby, PA: U.S. Department of Agriculture, Forest Service: 49–60.

Smith, P.D.; Merritt, M.; Nowak, D.; Hitchcock, D. 2005. Houston's Regional Forest. Structure, Functions, Values. Accessed via the World Wide Web at: <http://www.houstonregionalforest.org/Report/>> on 31 January 2006.

South Carolina Department of Health and Environmental Control. 2003. South Carolina stormwater management and sediment control handbook for land disturbance activities. Accessed on the World Wide Web at <http://www.scdhec.net/eqc/water/pubs/swmanual.pdf>.

Sullivan, W.C.; Kuo, E.E. 1996. Do trees strengthen urban communities, reduce domestic violence? Arborist News. 5(2):33–34.

Summit, J.; McPherson, E.G. 1998. Residential tree planting and care: a study of attitudes and behavior in Sacramento, California. J. Arboric. 24(2):89–97.

Sydnor, T.D.; Gamstetter, D.; Nichols, J.; Bishop, B.; Favorite, J.; Blazer, C.; Turpin, L. 2000. Trees are not the root of sidewalk problems. J.Arboric. 26:20–29.

Taha, H. 1996. Modeling impacts of increased urban vegetation on ozone air quality in the South Coast Air Basin. Atmospheric Environment. 30:3423–3420.

Thompson, R.P.; Ahern, J.J. 2000. The State of Urban and Community Forestry in California. San Luis Obispo, CA: Urban Forest Ecosystems Institute, California Polytechnic State University.

Tretheway, R.; Manthe, A. 1999. Skin cancer prevention: another good reason to plant trees. In: McPherson, E.G.; Mathis, S. (Eds.). Proceedings of the Best of the West Summit. Davis, CA: University of California, Davis:72–75.

Tyrvainen, L. 1999. Monetary Valuation of Urban Forest Amenities in Finland. Research Paper 739. Vantaa, Finland: Finnish Forest Research Institute. 129 pp.

Ulrich, R.S. 1985. Human responses to vegetation and landscapes. Landscape and Urban Planning. 13:29-44.

Urban, J. 1992. Bringing order to the technical dysfunction within the urban forest. J. Arboric. 18(2):85-90.

U.S. Census Bureau. 2005. Metropolitan and Micropolitan Statistical Areas. Population Estimates. Accessed via the World Wide Web at <http://www.census.gov/popest/metro.html> in June 2005.

U.S. Environmental Protection Agency. 1998. Ap-42 Compilation of Air Pollutant Emission Factors. 5th Edition. Volume I. Research Triangle Park, NC.

U.S. Environmental Protection Agency. 2003. E-GRID (E-GRID2002 Edition). Accessed via the World Wide Web <http://www.epa.gov/cleanenergy/egrid/index.htm> in June 2005.

U.S. Environmental Protection Agency. 2005. Green book: nonattainment areas for criteria pollutants. Accessed via the World Wide Web <http://www.epa.gov/oar/oaqps/greenbk/index.html> on May 2, 2005.

Wang, M.Q.; Santini, D.J. 1995. Monetary values of air pollutant emissions in various U.S. regions. Transportation Research Record. 1475:33–41.

Watson, G.W.; Himelick, E.B. 1997. Principles and practice of planting trees and shrubs. Savoy, IL: International Society of Arboriculture. 199 pp.

Wolf, K.L., 1999. Nature and commerce: human ecology in business districts. In: Kollin, C. (Ed.). Building Cities of Green: Proceedings of the 1999 National Urban Forest Conference. Washington, DC: American Forests: 56–59.

Xcelenergy 2004. Minnesota Electric Rate Book - Mpuc No. 2. Accessed via the World Wide Web <http://www.xcelenergy.com/docs/corpcomm/Me_Section_5.pdf> on Sept 12, 2004.

Xiao, Q.; McPherson, E.G. 2002. Rainfall interception by Santa Monica's municipal urban forest. Urban Ecosystems. 6:291–302.

Xiao, Q.; McPherson, E.G.; Simpson, J.R.; Ustin, S.L. 1998. Rainfall interception by Sacramento's urban forest. J. Arboric. 24(4):235–244.

Xiao, Q.; McPherson, E.G.; Simpson, J.R.; Ustin, S.L. 2000. Winter rainfall interception by two mature open grown trees in Davis, California. Hydrological Processes. 14(4):763–784.

www.ingramcontent.com/pod-product-compliance
Lightning Source LLC
Chambersburg PA
CBHW080314290526
45790CB00005B/2030